Praise for *I'm Right and You're a*

This is a deeply thoughtful book about what it ~~really takes to com~~municate, especially with people who we don't understand. A mustread for anyone trying to break the climate impasse, or indeed, make progress in any domain of social conflict.

NAOMI ORESKES, Professor of the History of Science, Affiliated Professor of Earth and Planetary Sciences, Harvard University

Learning how to protect the real freedoms we have in our caring society, James Hoggan brings critical insight into how we can have meaningful discourse where we carefully listen and not just hear words. With the political developments in many of our Western democracies, this book is particularly important and relevant. It is an incredibly important read.

ART VERLIEB, Q.C., Former President,
Law Society of British Columbia

As a popularizer of science, I had long assumed the more information people have, the better their actions and decisions. But today the public has unprecedented access to information, yet clearly political, economic and social policies are distorted by other factors. James Hoggan's monumental study explores a wide range of thought about the babel that passes for public discourse today. Anyone concerned about how civil society can be better informed so decisions can be made for the public's long term interests must read this deeply thoughtful book.

—DAVID SUZUKI, science broadcaster and environmental activist

In my experience in the world's crisis zones, inflammatory, toxic discourse exacerbates problems, creating conflict rather than resolving it — and probably gets you killed. So if you want to stay alive, read this incisive book. Honest engagement combined with a healthy dose of empathy is a far better route to constructive dialogue — and survival.

—NIGEL FISHER, humanitarian, former
UN Assistant Secretary General

James Hoggan reminds us that intelligent, meaningful public discourse on seemingly intractable issues such as climate change is necessary to develop consequential solutions—and why we are not there yet. His narrative points the way as to how to move from the barrier of headline-inducing conflict to the bridge of thoughtful deliberation, moving beyond facts and fanfare to values and vision as drivers of meaningful change. Public narratives need to change and *"I'm Right..."* shows us why and how.

TAMARA VROOMAN, President and CEO, Vancity

Hoggan writes superbly about the power of argumentation to strengthen democracy and advance social justice, and how it is so easily manipulated in pursuit of greed, power and politics. This is a must-read for anyone tired of the bullying, the propagandizing, the screaming and the bullsh*t.

—DR. SAMANTHA NUTT, author,
Damned Nations: Greed, Guns, Armies and Aid

This book should be required reading for every person engaged in the most polarizing issues of our time—whether it be climate change, healthcare, or global conflicts.

—JOHN RUFFOLO, CEO, OMERS Ventures

James Hoggan's book could not be more timely. At a moment when public discourse has seemingly deteriorated to the point of meaninglessness, the field abandoned to those who can simply yell the loudest, his call to tune down the volume, tone down the rhetoric and re-engage in civil, fact-based dialogue is more than important, it's crucial. Possibly our last hope of salvation. The fact this collection was curated by a public relations specialist is interesting; the depth and breadth of the ideas he challenges us with is impressive and ultimately inspiring. A must-read for anyone who despairs at the pollution in the public square. It doesn't have to be this way, says Hoggan. There is a way out.

—GILLIAN FINDLAY, Host, CBC News: the fifth estate

Conversation is the essence of being human. To converse is to listen, to respect, to love and so to be open to fresh ideas and perspectives. James Hoggan has illuminated a series of amazing conversations with thinkers and doers. His theme is that we all too easily create antagonism and deafness by organizing debates which punish rather than reveal the truth. If the eastern heart and the western mind are fused in honest conversation, the politics of antagonism which dominate almost every dialogue these days, would become the creativity of innovation. This is a text which should be thought, not just read, by all who seek reconciliation.

—Professor Tim O'Riordan
OBE DL FBA

Everyone, regardless of their politics, can learn something from this book. *I'm Right and You're an Idiot* steps into the frenzied space of public discourse where hyperbole and polarization rule the day. With sound insights and by pulling from the wisdom of spiritual and intellectual leaders from across disciplines, Hoggan charts a compelling and much needed path forward. *I'm Right and You're an Idiot* should be taught in every major in university... in every country of the world.

—Evangeline Lilly, author and actor

As if the world's many forms of social distress and environmental damage were not worrisome enough, we struggle even to communicate civilly with each other about these topics. James Hoggan has interviewed a diverse group of thinkers, from pundits to psychologists, seeking explanations of and alternatives to the all-too-familiar "stubborn adversarial advocacy" that pervades public discourse. This engaging and important book offers a blueprint toward empathy, flexibility, and creativity instead of narrow-minded demagoguery.

—Scott Slovic, co-editor, *Numbers and Nerves:*
Information, Emotion, and Meaning in a World of Data

Impressive list of contributors; important topic; inspired insights.

—BRENDA MORRISON, Ph.D, Director,
Centre for Restorative Justice, Simon Fraser University

Hoggan has done an admirable job in getting to the root of the why public discourse on some of the most pressing problems facing society today is so fractured and toxic. His interviews with many of the world's leading thinkers on this crucial issue are essential reading for anyone who wants to understand how we got into this mess and what we can do to get out of it.

MARK JACCARD, Professor, School of Resource and
Environmental Management, Simon Fraser University

Jim Hoggan has spent decades shaping public discourse. It's fitting, therefore, that his new book draws on the knowledge of some of the world's leading thinkers to focus new attention on why the state of public discourse has become so toxic and what we can do to clean it up.

I'm Right, and You're An Idiot is essential reading for anyone who is concerned about the deterioration of public discourse and our inability to engage constructively on the social, political and environmental problems we all face.

STEPHEN BRONFMAN, Executive Chairman, Claridge Inc.

I'm Right and You're an Idiot

THE TOXIC STATE OF PUBLIC DISCOURSE AND HOW TO CLEAN IT UP

James Hoggan

with Grania Litwin

new society
PUBLISHERS

Cover design by Diane McIntosh.
Cover image © iStock

Printed in Canada. Second printing July 2016.

Funded by the   Financé par le
Government   gouvernement
of Canada   du Canada

Paperback ISBN: 978-0-86571-817-3
eISBN: 978-1-55092-612-5

Inquiries regarding requests to reprint all or part of *I'm Right and You're an Idiot*
should be addressed to New Society Publishers at the address below.
To order directly from the publishers, please call toll-free (North America)
1-800-567-6772, or order online at www.newsociety.com

Any other inquiries can be directed by mail to:

New Society Publishers
P.O. Box 189, Gabriola Island, BC V0R 1X0, Canada
(250) 247-9737

LIBRARY AND ARCHIVES CANADA CATALOGUING IN PUBLICATION

Hoggan, James, 1946-, author
I'm right and you're an idiot : the toxic state of public discourse and how to clean it up /
James Hoggan with Grania Litwin.

Includes bibliographical references and index.
Issued in print and electronic formats.
ISBN 978-0-86571-817-3 (paperback).—ISBN 978-1-55092-612-5 (ebook)

1. Interpersonal communication. 2. Debates and debating.
3. Polarization (Social sciences). I. Litwin, Grania, author II. Title.

III. Title: I'm right and you're an idiot.

HM1166.H64 2016   302.2   C2016-900789-8
                                        C2016-900790-1

New Society Publishers' mission is to publish books that contribute in fundamental ways
to building an ecologically sustainable and just society, and to do so with the least possible
impact on the environment, in a manner that models this vision. We are committed to doing
this not just through education, but through action. The interior pages of our bound books
are printed on Forest Stewardship Council®-registered acid-free paper that is 100% post-
consumer recycled (100% old growth forest-free), processed chlorine-free, and printed with
vegetable-based, low-VOC inks, with covers produced using FSC®-registered stock. New
Society also works to reduce its carbon footprint, and purchases carbon offsets based on
an annual audit to ensure a carbon neutral footprint. For further information, or to browse
our full list of books and purchase securely, visit our website at: www.newsociety.com

MIX
Paper from
responsible sources
FSC® C016245

Contents

SECTION C: Duped and How

Part II: Speak the Truth, But Not to Punish

SECTION D: Leaning Into the Future

SECTION E: The Mighty Tool of Public Narrative

SECTION F: From the Heart

Acknowledgments

Five years ago when I started the journey to write this book I had no idea how long and difficult the road would be. The scope of the project became massive. The more I researched and the more people I spoke to, the more I realized that I had to draw a line somewhere and tell myself to stop. Having the opportunity to interview some of the world's leading thinkers on the issues I have explored in the book was an exhilarating privilege, but it was also painful at times. It opened my eyes to the very difficult task we face in moving towards a level of public discourse that will allow us to discuss and resolve the most critical issues of our time. Everyone I interviewed added to my own knowledge and understanding. I would not have succeeded without their insights and guidance. Many of them are featured in the book and the views of others are on the website www.imrightand youreanidiot.com. Those who I have not quoted in the book contributed nonetheless by helping guide me to the final product and I thank them all most sincerely.

This book began with an almost impossible question and endless curiosity about its answer. I would never have been able to come close to finding that answer without the support, encouragement, advice and friendship of many people.

Grania Litwin, who helped me transform the interviews and my jumbled thoughts into eloquent prose, is a very special person. What she thought would be a one-year project turned into a four-year commitment, but she never wavered. And just as important as her writing and editing skills was her real-world view that kept me focused as we worked through the massive volume of information I had gathered in the interviews. Thank you Grania; I was blessed to have found you.

I had the great fortune early on in the project of attracting the interest of Ashley Arden, one of the smartest young people I have ever met. As my thought partner and fellow adventurer, Ashley contributed invaluable research, assisted with interviews and helped guide me in the right direction. She also told me when to stop, or I might still be travelling the world doing interviews.

I also owe a debt of considerable gratitude to my friend Alex Himelfarb whose thoughtful advice and generosity of spirit through many stages of the project added shape and meaning to the book.

To Nick Anderson for his forthright guidance and for nudging me to focus on rhetoric, and for introducing me to the work of Bruno Latour.

And to my long-suffering executive assistant, Kirsten Brynelsen, who successfully battled the chaos and knuckled down to learn new skills like editing, social media, website development, infographics, marketing, etc., etc., etc.

I also thank my long-time friends and supporters David Suzuki and Tara Cullis for their ongoing encouragement and guidance.

To the team at DeSmogBlog; Brendan Demelle, Carol Linnitt, Emma Gilchrist and Brendan Montague, for their research and dedication to the important work they do and for being the book project's catalyst.

I didn't interview Debra Tannen, but I studied some of her vast body of work on linguistics to help me understand how the language of everyday conversation affects relationships. I found her book, *Argument Culture, Stopping Americans War of Words*, particularly helpful. I also borrowed her quote, *Smashing Heads Doesn't Open Minds*, as the title for Section A of the book. Thank you Debra for inspiring me.

Thank you also to friends and colleagues who very generously gave up their time to read an early draft of the book that had no right to see the light of day. You helped identify the gems buried deep inside those 120,000 words and provided thoughtful advice on how I could make the book better: Ed Levy, Emma Gilchrist, Nancy McHarg, Peter Robinson, Chris Hatch, John Lefebvre, Chris Freimond and Freydis Welland.

Apart from reading the early draft, John Lefebvre was a constant source of generous support. His wisdom and sage advice on the state of public discourse kept me on track. Thank you my friend.

Thanks to Emma Pullman for support in the early stages of the project, and to Simon Kelly for his research skills and to Gary Ross, who helped with the title as we moved to the conclusion.

Most of all, I am grateful to my wife, Enid Marion. Without her quiet patience, loyal support and endless enthusiasm for what I was trying to achieve, I would never have concluded what became such a time-consuming and costly distraction from our normal life. Thank you Enid from the bottom of my heart.

Prologue

The environment is not the main subject of this book.

But a seed was planted more than a decade ago, shortly after I was appointed to the board of the David Suzuki Foundation, Canada's best known science-based environmental organization. I was invited to join because of my experience as a public affairs consultant. After my first board meeting we all adjourned to dinner at a French bistro in Old Montreal, where I was seated across from David Suzuki. The board members at our end of the table were having a lively conversation about the lack of action on environmental problems when Suzuki looked at me and asked one of his famously blunt, straight-to-the-heart-of-the-matter questions: "Why aren't people paying more attention? There is enough evidence we are destroying the planet. Why aren't people out in the streets? How do we motivate the public to demand action?"

A silence followed and I didn't produce much of an answer, but the question struck a chord with me for two reasons: First, because I was talking to "Mr. Standing Ovation." David Suzuki is an inspiring speaker, one of the world's great environmental educators, and here he was asking my advice and expressing frustration at not being able to motivate people. That was very humbling.

Second, since hanging out my public relations shingle in 1984 I have dealt with all kinds of prickly, front-page, public relations controversies and crisis situations—food poisonings, labor disputes, market crashes, animal cruelty charges, bodies disappearing from funeral homes, Taser deaths, multimillion dollar bank fraud, exploding sawmills, election and sex scandals—and I'm seen as one of the gurus in my field. But this was a communication dilemma of a different class, and the question baffled me. I remember muttering something about the state of politics as I fumbled for an answer, but the truth was I had no idea.

Over the next few years, I became interested in the role that misinformation and pseudoscience play in this change resistance problem, and the ways in which manufactured doubt and controversy can be used to stall the growth of public concern and block public policy solutions. In 2006 I co-founded DeSmogBlog[1] to help dispel the public relations fog that swirls around climate science and global warming, to raise awareness and help people become more savvy about the problem of spin. It has gained millions of readers and was named as one of the best blogs of 2011 by *Time* magazine. In 2009 I wrote *Climate Cover-Up* with Richard Littlemore,[2] to take a deeper look at science propaganda and the widespread echo chamber of media and think tanks that magnify it. The book became a Canadian bestseller, was translated into Mandarin and reprinted in Spanish, yet I was shocked that people were not more outraged by all the evidence of deception.

So, several years ago I set out to write a follow-up book which I planned to call *Duped and How*. I wanted to take a deeper look at the history and techniques of propaganda, but as I began doing interviews it became painfully clear that misinformation campaigns and propaganda are only part of the problem. I was pointed in the direction of one of the most urgent and unexamined human relations problems of our time: pollution in the public square, that literal and figurative place where we assemble to talk freely and debate honestly, where we seek truth without recrimination, whether on a street corner, in a blog, campus hall, political meeting, bulletin board or actual community square. How can we make space for real public conversations? How have we come to a time when facts don't matter, and how can we begin the journey back to where they do? I was also keen to discover what kinds of conversations can actually change people's minds about what's possible, about what's desirable and about where their personal responsibility lies. This is not a book about creating campaigns to change people's behavior as consumers or voters. It isn't about persuading people to become environmentalists or prodding them to take action. This book is about something much more fundamental. It's about the threshold of change, and how we create the space for higher-quality public debates where passionate opposition and science shape constructive, mind-changing conversations.

I have interviewed political pundits, philosophers, moral psychologists, media gurus and social scientists, and have found that the intellectual environment is ripe for this discussion. They all agree that polluted public discourse is an enormous obstacle to change—and many of them have been looking into some aspect of this problem for a long time, some for their entire careers.

During the early interviews I came to understand, as Yale Law School professor Dan Kahan put it, that "just as we can pollute the natural environment, we can pollute public conversations."[3] While the experts disagree about why this is happening, they concur when it comes to the damage it does: toxic conversations stall our ability to think collectively and solve the many dangerous problems that are stalking everyone on Earth.

✦ ✦ ✦ ✦ ✦

I have divided the book into two sections. Part I: The Polluted Public Square explains how we create toxic dialogue and how we might turn down the noise and open up the space needed for healthy conversations. It looks at barriers to change, what blocks healthy public discourse and some of the main sources of the pollution. We see how the advocacy that is needed to draw attention to these issues can become a combative, polarized debate that often drives us into gridlock and shoving matches; how a mistaken confidence in the power of facts leads to narrative failure; and how propaganda can destroy public discussion and eradicate understanding.

Part II: Speak the Truth But Not to Punish investigates how we can have more constructive conversations. This section describes how we can change our style of public communication and improve human relations. We learn about the latest techniques of conflict resolution, gain insights into the power of moral narrative and realize how educating the heart can bring about deeper awareness and understanding. This division is a general structure, and readers will note that many experts touch on both challenges and solutions.

David Suzuki's question stirred up weighty conversations and sage advice from experts such as Columbia University's Eric Johnson, a behavioral economist who rephrased the question: "Why isn't public discourse on the environment more data driven, and why are we listening to each other shout instead of listening to what the evidence is trying to tell us?"[4]

Linguistics professor Deborah Tannen points out that smashing heads won't open minds. She suggests that our habit of attacking the motives and character of those who disagree with us distracts the public from the real issues and undermines genuine opposition as it discredits the passion and outrage at the heart of real public debate. "Accusing opponents of venal motives makes it easy to dismiss valid criticism." She believes that this combative style of public debate leaves little room for the middle ground, and what's worse, "when extremes define the issues, problems seem insoluble and citizens become alienated from the political process."[5]

Caustic dialogue is not limited to issues of the environment or climate change. The problem is evident whether people are talking about immigration, gun control or immunization, and it comes from all quarters, including advocates, elected officials and industry groups.

It would be naïve to suggest that the only reasons we fail to take action on the serious problems we face is polarized debate, aggressive rhetoric or pollution in the public square. Nor is it merely a matter of information deficit. The inertia that Suzuki pointed to can be blamed, in part, on the scope and scale of problems such as ocean acidification, species extinction and climate change, which is the mother of all systems problems. As French philosopher Bruno Latour explained, solving this critical situation will require seven billion people to completely transform almost every aspect of their lives. So it's small wonder there is change resistance.

As a PR specialist I have spent 30 years dealing with tough issues, straddling the worlds of government and industry, business and the environment, and I see this dysfunctional dialogue and corruption in the public square as not only a pressing problem, but also a threshold problem. If we don't find a way to work this out, to disagree more constructively, we may never arrive at timely solutions to critical collective problems. When faced with an onslaught of over-the-top advocacy, not to mention corrupt or inept conversations, people lose interest, lose hope or simply lose the thread of what they're being told. And this leads to escalating polarization and eventually to gridlock.

Based on current evidence, more than 97 percent of peer-reviewed papers by the world's climate scientists have found that human activity is contributing to global warming[6] and yet our counter-evolutionary behavior is going unchecked. Instead of weighing facts fairly, disagreeing constructively and thinking things through cooperatively, we have forces at work to halt the vital steps we should take to save our precious ecosystems. We need vigorous debate and people speaking out with passion.

Vigorous discussion and debate are necessary in a healthy democracy, and we have to defend that right while protecting our public square for generations to come. This imperative reminds me of the famous tragedy of Guernica, poignantly captured in Picasso's painting of the same name. In 1937 the German Luftwaffe bombed this small town in northern Spain, but by some miracle an oak tree in the town square survived. Ever since Guernica was founded in 1366 that tree, or its descendent, had stood in the town square, and under its branches citizens gathered to create laws, swear oaths of fealty and discuss community matters. Whenever the tree became sick, another sapling grown from its acorn was planted in its place, because residents valued and understood its symbolic role in the community. Although the aerial bombardment caused widespread death and destruction, the town's freedom tree survived along with the spirit of its people. We need to protect our public square from the bombardment of propaganda, polarization and failed communication.

PART I

The Polluted Public Square

The public square is that literal and symbolic place where we meet to discuss and debate problems of the commons. It may be a church basement, a television studio or around a water cooler, but most importantly the public square is a place where citizens gather to discuss important community matters, governance and participate in democracy.

Our public squares should be forums for open and honest, higher-quality debate, but sadly, these meeting places have become polluted by a toxic mix of polarized rhetoric, propaganda and miscommunication. A dark haze of unyielding one-sidedness has poisoned public discourse and created an atmosphere of mistrust and disinterest. In this first part of *I'm Right* we will examine how we all pollute the public square, and how we can make space for healthier dialogue.

Smashing Heads Doesn't Open Minds

1

Like Ships In the Night

with DANIEL YANKELOVICH

W HEN I FIRST BEGAN thinking about writing this book I invited Steve Rosell to lunch at a little Italian restaurant across
the bay from San Francisco in Sausalito, California. I wanted his
reaction to my early thoughts. I also wanted to convince him that
my ideas were worthy of an interview with his famous colleague,
social scientist Daniel Yankelovich. I had first met Daniel Yankelovich more than a decade earlier. I had read his brilliant books and
valued his thinking tremendously. Born in 1924, Yankelovich is the
author of 12 books and has held professorships or other academic
affiliations with New York University, the graduate faculty of the
New School for Social Research, the University of California, and
Harvard University.[1] Together, Rosell and Yankelovich are pioneers
in an evolving field that uses dialogue to deal with highly polarized
public conflict.

During my lunch with Rosell I mentioned I was considering calling my next book *Duped and How,* and he immediately expressed
concern that such an inflammatory title would set the book up, right
at the outset, as a polarizing piece of work. Starting with a title that
seems to say "I'm right and you're an idiot" is not the best way to
influence people or help them move toward considered judgment,
said Rosell, who has a doctoral degree from Cornell, has been an

advisor to numerous international agencies, major corporations and has worked with four Canadian Prime Ministers.[2]

Rosell emphasized his point by recalling the 2011 debt ceiling crisis in Washington DC, when everyone argued up until the last minute. This kind of debate, or "debacle" as Rosell called it, is totally ineffective and seemed to him like a stalled airplane was hurtling toward Earth while everyone in the cockpit argued about what to do. Rosell said conspiracy theorists assume there is a clever plan behind such combative exchanges, but the scarier truth is that when it comes to today's political posturing there is no great and clever plan: "Nobody is pulling the strings. It's just out of control," he said.

I was conflicted by this conversation. On one hand I was reluctant to change the title I proposed because I was angry about the pervasive propaganda and underhanded public relations trickery I was witnessing, deceit that conceals the gravity of so many environmental issues. Few speak out about this dark art, and I was keen to expose its perils, the spell it casts over unsuspecting victims. At the same time, how could I dismiss his wisdom? Rosell argued that assuming this stance would slam the door on many thoughtful, open-minded readers.

Later, I realized that by starting out with a polarizing position and aggressive posture emblazoned across the cover of my book, I could ironically and precisely illustrate the conflict-heavy tone I disapprove of. So thank you, Steve, for the title.

I wanted to hear the reactions of these two social scientists to David Suzuki's question, and also learn more about the power of dialogue, how to mend broken conversations and achieve clear, collaborative communication so we can triangulate issues in innovative ways and find creative solutions. I was interested in their thoughts about the state of public discourse, propaganda, polarization, activism and the work I had described in my book *Climate Cover-Up*.[3]

Rosell set up the interview,[4] we three sat down together in San Diego, and Yankelovich got right to the point when he said polarization is dangerous because it interrupts lines of communication

**We have an almost extreme situation
where the very intelligent elites are
sort of mumbling, and bumbling,
and proceeding as if they were
communicating—when they're not.**

DANIEL YANKELOVICH

and leads to gridlock. It stops us from tackling urgent problems because without consensus we cannot take effective action. Rather than highlighting our differences, he said we should be working toward finding common ground, and moving into a place where we can reserve judgment until we have considered other ways to approach controversial issues.

Yankelovich once wrote: "Democracy requires space for compromise, and compromise is best won through acknowledging the legitimate concerns of the other. We need to bridge opposing positions, not accentuate differences."[5] He added that any unyielding one-sidedness creates a mood of corrosive bitterness. Worst of all, it is a formula for losing the battle, whether it's a war on terror or combating global warming. Taking a polarized attitude toward critical issues will inevitably yield answers that are dogmatic—and wrong—and keep us from arriving at truth.

"It's sad to say, but our culture favors debate, advocacy and conflict over dialogue and deliberation," Yankelovich said. These adversarial forms of discourse have their uses when attacking special interests in a courtroom or on television when we want our talking heads to be entertaining, but they're the wrong way to cope with the gridlock that threatens to paralyze our society. He said today's typical model of mass communication—"where people are not listening, being mistrustful, being polarized, not sharing the same basic understandings or mental frameworks"—distorts any possible discussion. We desperately need to find common ground.

Yankelovich believes the quality of public discourse today is "very poor" partly because people are generally inattentive to public affairs and because the media plays by its own rules. In addition, our public discourse is undermined by a lack of understanding about the rules of communication.

In particular, the scientific community is largely innocent of the rules of public discourse. So we have very gifted experts offering abstract, technical, difficult, highly qualified statements, and a media that presents what these people say in the form of controversy. "And since it involves an awful lot of inconvenience, people prefer to ignore it, saying, 'If you people can't agree, what do you expect of us?'"

The scientific community assumes the same rules of communication are always applicable and rational, that people are attentive, open-minded, persuaded by facts and believe that those who are presenting information are people of goodwill, and not deliberately trying to manipulate them. But none of those things are true.

Communicating under conditions of mistrust requires a different approach, said Yankelovich, who spent the first 30 years of his career in market research. Under these circumstances the first step is to acknowledge the skepticism or concern people feel, and then encourage them to reason why in this particular instance it isn't applicable. The approach should be: the burden of proof is on us; performance should exceed expectations; promises should be few and faithfully kept; core values must be made explicit and framed in ethical terms; anything but plain talk is suspect; all bearing in mind that noble goals with flawed execution will be seen as hypocrisy, not idealism.

When dealing with conditions of inattention the objective is obvious: get people to listen. If they are mistrustful at the start, they won't listen, even to fair and balanced points of view by distinguished and credible scientists. So a key place to begin thinking about this is for policy makers and scientists to recognize that communication is not going on when they think it is. "We have an almost extreme situation where the very intelligent elites are sort of mumbling, and bumbling, and proceeding as if they were communicating—when they're not."

Yankelovich explained that university professors are used to communicating under conditions of trust and assuming the public knows they act in good faith and will therefore accept their version of things. Well that's not true either, said the expert. Communicating under conditions of mistrust and political polarization is very different than communicating under conditions of trust. When we understand these elements—inattention, mistrust and polarization—it's clear why the truth about global warming has become so distorted.

Yankelovich added that the advertising profession has developed ways to communicate under conditions of mistrust and inattention, and others should too.

This is also where authentic conversation comes in. Yankelovich believes dialogue is not an arcane and esoteric intellectual exercise. It is a practical, everyday tool that is accessible to all, and when we use dialogue rather than debate we gain completely different insights into the ways people see the world. Those who say they are "dialogued out" on topics such as terrorism or pipelines are actually tired of the lack of real dialogue, because most dialogue is just disguised monologue.

During our interviews, Yankelovich and Rosell explained the clear differences between dialogue and debate: in debate we assume we have the right answer, whereas dialogue assumes we all have pieces of the answer and can craft a solution together. Debate is combative and about winning, while dialogue is collaborative and focuses on exploring the common good. Debaters defend their assumptions and criticize the views of others, whereas in dialogue we reveal assumptions and reexamine all positions, including our own.

I especially appreciated their comment that debate is about seeing weaknesses in other people's positions, while dialogue is about searching for strength and value in our opponents' concerns. This means approaching environmental issues with an open-minded attitude that we could be wrong and others could be right.

Yankelovich stressed that the special form of communication called *dialogue* is only needed when people don't share the same framework, when ordinary conversation fails and people are passing each other "like ships in the night." Authentic dialogue takes some effort to achieve and would not be worth the trouble if we could communicate more simply. In other words, when everybody is singing off the same sheet, shares the same values, goals and framework, we can all communicate just fine. But when we have highly educated scientists communicating with poorly educated citizens, as well as policy makers, people from the oil industry and stakeholders, it's obvious that everybody brings a different frame to the issue.

Climate change is a perfect storm when it comes to communication, because it involves a broad array of stakeholders, people with differing values, frameworks and levels of education—all being whipped up by winds of passion and emotion. Rosell added that a growing gap between elites and the general public breeds mistrust between those different universes of discourse. "Government folks talk in jargon, and scientists talk about data. The public talks a different language, and you have to earn their trust. You can't assume trust anymore."

In our lawyer-ridden society the dominant mode of communication is advocacy, Yankelovich observed. Advocates are trying to sell something, whereas dialogue needs people who will listen, pay attention and suspend judgment so there is enough shared framework that even if people disagree, they can find some common ground.

When I asked Yankelovich how he became absorbed in the world of dialogue, he described an interesting journey. After having trained in philosophy and psychology, he moved into market research and public opinion polling, but was disappointed in the level of public discourse and the fact people rarely gave thoughtful, considered responses. He noticed this kind of "raw" opinion has certain structural characteristics. For one thing, it is full of contradictions. Ask people the same question at different times and you get different answers. Change the wording slightly and answers change again. People's views are inconsistent and, most importantly, people don't tend to think through the consequences of their views.

Having isolated these characteristics, Yankelovich determined to find out under what conditions people could move from raw opinion to more thoughtful judgment, where their views would be consistent and where they would be aware of the consequences. In the course of trying to answer these questions, he came upon dialogue, and that led to his ongoing work on how to improve the quality of public discourse and public trust.

Yankelovich and Rosell have identified a process they call *the public learning curve* that describes maturing public opinions, where people's views evolve from poorly informed reactions to more thoughtful conclusions. The three-stage process begins with building awareness and consciousness (where advocates and the media typically do a good job). The second stage involves working through wishful thinking and denial, resistance to change and mistrust, grasping at straws, deliberate obfuscation and lack of urgency (which is where dialogue comes in). The third part of the learning curve is when people come to resolution (which is handled by decision-makers and governance institutions). "Much of our work focuses on improving the 'working through' stage, which our society does not handle well and where critical issues like climate change can get stuck for years or decades," said Rosell.

The dialogue specialists have developed tools and techniques to accelerate this process, but it still takes time, and Rosell explained that's to be expected. Experts in all fields have taken many years to master a sphere of knowledge and understand an issue. "There is an assumption that somehow the public will do that instantly, but they don't. They need time to work through the learning curve, and it can take decades in some cases."

In conclusion Rosell emphasized: "Public discourse matters, public confidence matters and trust matters if you want to achieve anything collectively. But what's going on now is not competent, not effective, not legitimate and it's undermining public trust."

The ability to have an honest conversation is a tremendous national and public resource, but what Rosell sees happening now is a deliberate attempt to fracture society. We've all been exposed to this during election campaigns, when we hear outlandish attacks, out-of-control PR and distorted information, but Rosell said this conduct has a cost when it enters everyday life. "You keep doing that, and doing that, and you basically pollute the commons."

Protecting the public square and the public good is an objective worthy of support, he said, and by working to create a climate of trust, a community of discourse, we build up capital that we can use to deal with tricky issues in the future. On the other hand, when public conversations are corrupted, when we can't think things through because of a tangle of polarization, attack rhetoric and failure of experts to communicate, it is difficult if not impossible for people to move from raw to considered opinion. It is hard enough to go through these stages when we are exposed to clear arguments and healthy discourse, he said, and added that people can surprise themselves when they find common ground and manage to talk and disagree in a different way.

2

The Advocacy Trap

with ROGER CONNER

WHEN WE LOOK at the miserable state of public discourse today and how we are polluting the public square, it's plain to see that many people believe the problem derives from evil on "the other side." But this kind of pollution comes from all around the square—including our side—and as long as we think somebody else is the source of it, we're unlikely to ever see our way through it. The problem is structural and derives from human psychology, the way we look at the world and from ill-intentioned and well-intentioned sources alike. It also arises from the nature of advocacy.

My ideas about this book were still developing when I came across the work of lobbyist, litigator and consensus builder Roger Conner. Conner has spent close to half a century studying public discourse and now teaches a course on non-litigation strategies for social and political change at Vanderbilt Law School in Nashville, Tennessee. Conner told me that my pollution analogy is particularly apt when applied to climate change because smog was long believed to come from factories. Eventually we acknowledged the possibility that it was individual car drivers who were causing the greatest harm—a controversial view when first advanced.[1]

Conner says that most of us aren't evil, and good people sometimes do bad things for good reasons. If we don't understand that, we fall into something he calls *the advocacy trap*, which happens when we come to believe that people who disagree with us are wrongdoers. This judgment causes us to become locked into such a foe stance that we lose sight of our purpose. People can't collaborate to solve global or systemic problems when we treat one another as enemies.

Roger Conner acknowledged he spent the first part of his career as a "name 'em, blame 'em, shame 'em advocate" and thought he had learned everything he needed to know about advocacy in Sunday school: "There was David and Goliath, and I was always David. There was Moses and Pharaoh, and I was always Moses." What these biblical heroes did exceedingly well was identify the source of evil, name it and crush it.

Conner was caught up by that brilliant simplicity, and his first gig as an advocate was in the environmental movement, running the West Michigan Environmental Action Council. His motto there was, We fight evil and do good. But then Conner went to Washington DC to work on immigration issues and was in for a shock. He discovered a whole other cadre of people who thought that they were David and he was Goliath; "they wanted to destroy me," Conner realized. Still, he decided the way to be a successful advocate was to redouble his efforts to overcome his enemies. The media loved him, and soon Conner was appearing on every major talk show in the US and was a regular on CNN's *Crossfire*.

One day he was invited to the US National Institute of Justice to work on crime and disorder issues "at a time when big cities in the US were falling apart;" while working at the local level Conner had a eureka moment. For the first time in his life, he found his tried-and-true approach—identifying the correct solution, identifying the enemy and overcoming the enemy—didn't work. "If you're trying to get rid of a group of drug dealers, maybe that works. But you can't deal with police that way, or neighborhood organizations or the public defender." Conner went back to the drawing board and began earnestly researching local communities all around the US that were successfully tackling crime. In every instance, Roger Conner found people who were historically on the Left working effectively with people on the Right.

Solutions were evolving wherever members of the community and police worked collaboratively, where people were suspending areas of disagreement and seeking common goals. Perhaps most importantly, Conner realized it was impossible to understand the problems, let alone create solutions, without deeply hearing what people were saying. The result? At the end of his research Conner found himself "essentially unemployable," as he no longer believed in the effectiveness of any of his former advocacy tools.

The solution must lie in more peacemakers, Conner surmised, and for a decade he toiled as a professional peacemaker on public policy issues. But Conner realized the greater challenge was to create new, more sophisticated advocates. At Vanderbilt Law School, while consulting to a couple of foundations, Conner witnessed how many public policy issues devolved into shoving matches in which neither side fully understood the problem. He saw people blinded by their own resentments and hatred.

Conner set out to understand why this was happening and began reading works by people like Harvard public policy lecturer and author Marshall Ganz and Martin Luther King, "people who are less theoretical and more practical." Conner had previously thought that professional Washington lobbyists were bad people engaging in polarizing conduct, but then asked himself, "Could it be that we have good people doing bad things for good reasons?" On the whole, yes, he said, and he added this is at the root of polarized public discourse.

Concerning environmental campaigns against oil and gas pipelines in Canada, Conner admonished, "If you think that the whole movement of people advocating for the pipeline in Canada is made up of people who are either evil or idiots, I can almost assure you with great certainty that's not accurate."

I found his answer surprising and slightly irritating, but Connor sees effective advocacy as a way to change the flow of events in the public life of a community by altering the way key individuals and groups think, feel and act."The flow of events is complex, like a river with many tributaries," and the effective advocate seeks to alter that stream by guiding individuals and institutions to change their behavior.

Conner said there are two obvious ways to change behavior—by pushing and pulling—and one less obvious way involving collaboration. The push approach makes a person do something whether they want to or not, and the pull strategy involves cajoling someone through education, incentives or warnings. The third option operates like a well-functioning community team and entails solving specific problems through deep forms of collaboration in which participants may agree to disagree on other matters. The collaboration strategy requires all participants to step off their narrow paths, surrender individual egos and agendas. No one ever does it perfectly, and at first Conner thought these three fundamentals were the whole answer.

But it soon occurred to him there is another dimension. Conner calls it *stance*. Stance is about attitudes we hold toward another person or group, and allows us to describe others as friend or foe, from bosom buddies down the spectrum to bitter enemies. (Conner uses the term *friend* not in the sense of liking a person but to signify that we respect them and accept they are decent, even though they hold other opinions.)

Conner explained that the most common strategy when trying to overpower someone believed to have evil interests is push-foe, whereas push-friend would be utilized when working with a government official or legislator who agrees with you. Pushing in this instance is done from a place of respect and care. You wouldn't want to cause this person to lose her or his job. You wouldn't call them names. A pull-friend or collaboration-friend strategy is usually stable and sustained over time, as is a foe-push strategy. Why in the latter case? Because unfortunately, most of us have attitudes toward other people or groups that are determined by their behavior toward us."If you behave like my enemy, I understand you are my enemy." If you behave like a self-interested, profit-seeking, care-nothing-for-

**There are a few profoundly evil people
in the world, but if you think you're
surrounded by them, you probably need
to change your own psyche.**

ROGER CONNER

the-environment person and call me a liar, I see you as my enemy,
Conner said. So we commonly allow our stance to be determined by
other people's behavior.

This leads to what Conner calls the advocacy trap. People don't
start out as enemies—it happens in stages. When people disagree
with us, we first question their views, but eventually we question
their motives and intentions. When they persist in their disagreement with us, we start to perceive them as aggressors. When they
criticize our cause or condemn our reasoning, our defense mechanisms kick in. We are offended and start to get angry. When both
sides in an argument draw their stance from the perceived behavior
of the other, people eventually start treating each other as not just
wrong, but as wrongdoer, and then as enemies. Once that happens, it
is almost impossible to do anything over a sustained period of time
other than futilely push one another.

Conner observed that the advocacy trap is very much like other
seductive but ultimately self-destructive pleasures. In the short run it
provides attention, "from the all-important media and applause, not
to mention money, from their base, but in the long run this behavior
prevents them [advocates] from fulfilling the calling that drew them
into public advocacy in the first place."

Effective advocates need to shift from push, to collaborate, to pull
as circumstances change. It's very difficult to engage in genuine collaboration or even compromise with someone you consider untrustworthy, evil or despicable. In a sustained dispute, if both parties draw
their impressions from the perceived behavior of the other, each of

them mirrors what they think the other is doing. It doesn't take long for them to look at each other with profound distrust. Once the advocacy trap is set, breaking the circle of blame is extraordinarily difficult. To escape this rancorous circle an advocate needs to stand up and walk away. In three decades of experience Conner has seen no other solution to such inflamed situations. To explicitly and consciously choose a stance of respect, or better yet empathy and compassion—and to do so without expectation of reciprocity, is exceedingly hard. But letting go of the foe stance can break a stalemate.

Conner does not suggest people stop fighting for what they believe in, but he counsels us all to police our attitudes so we can learn to push sometimes, pull sometimes, collaborate sometimes, and remain limber enough to sway back and forth, like a light-footed boxer, as the situation demands. Too much aggression will automatically and absolutely increase the energy the other side is devoting to an issue, Conner explained. "Nothing's so common as powerful groups creating resistance by overplaying their hands and dealing in ungenerous or resentful ways."

Roger Conner, who is also a consultant on advocacy strategies, conflict resolution and polarization, said it takes conscious thought and discipline to generate our attitudes toward others from the inside, rather than having them develop from the outside. But people who monitor their attitudes toward others, and don't allow resentment to boil up, can actually hear what others are saying. A good police officer employs that skill so an angry drunk can't provoke them. A wise doctor does not become emotionally upset when a child with multiple gunshot wounds comes into the ER. Parents do this too, when raising children. Of course, some kids are smart enough to get under their parents' skins, but a smart parent can overcome that, just as a good CEO does. Few of us practice this skill of not letting our perceptions control our attitudes, and as a result we hand over control of a vital part of our cognitive machinery to someone else.

In a 2005 paper entitled "Strategy and Stance,"[2] Conner said a leader such as Martin Luther King refused to fall into the advocacy trap because he refused to allow his stance to be a reflection of the behavior of others. He did not give others the right or the power to determine his attitude. The same was true of Mahatma Gandhi, who refused to hate those who imprisoned him. To use the entire range of strategic options, a public advocate must avoid thinking of others as foes.

Conner observed that it is no surprise that good people do bad things for good reasons. And the advocacy trap is to be expected in a political arena where people disagree, just as it's normal for a swamp to stink at night. "But what has changed in the current environment, compared to when I first started 40 or 50 years ago, is the increasing number of people involved in advocacy." Sheer volume is creating more polarization as more people are treating one another as enemies.

The antidote is to develop a greater capacity for self-awareness and self-control, because "resentment is like a drug. It feels good to go home and say: 'Those assholes! Those jerks! Those liberals. Those conservatives... I'm right, they're wrong.'" Self-righteousness becomes a fuel that can justify "damn near anything." Conner has seen how resentment escalates in groups that start out only mildly resentful of each other. Discussion grows about how the other side is misusing information or ways in which they're making unjust attacks. "The truth is we all have some degree of uncertainty, and we go to this self-righteous place to protect ourselves from that uncertainty." Righteous indignation is necessary to act in the face of injustice, but self-righteousness develops when you cannot admit there may an error in your point of view—or the possibility the other side is motivated by something other than evil. "I believe it's possible to think somebody is completely wrong, but also to believe they are a decent person who has somehow got it wrong." If you can hold that thought, you will avoid falling into the advocacy trap.

In conclusion, Conner urges advocates to abandon the foe stance and hold every person in their vision with respect. If you need to do it for religious reasons by saying every person is a child of God, try that. If you need to do it for psychological reasons and say, "I don't know what childhood experiences this person had that led them to behave this way," try that. Start by assuming others' intentions are good, and believing the leader of an organization deserves respect.

In Conner's experience, it's better to be clearheaded and respectful when pushing a strategy. It leads to greater understanding. Push strategies are often essential to wake someone up, but you need to switch to pull and then move toward collaboration as soon as possible. Success comes from understanding another's needs so fully that you can reshape the future together.

3

Mistakes Were Made
(But Not By Me)

with CAROL TAVRIS

AFTER LISTENING TO Roger Conner explain how people base their stance on the perceived behavior of others, I wanted to learn more about what it is in our human nature that makes us stumble again and again into these advocacy traps. What drives good people to do bad things? What fuels human beings' obstinate behavior, irrational justification and confrontational opinions in the face of convincing arguments and information? I needed to understand more about how people form opinions and how the process of self-justification is a controlling psychological force, a huge barrier to communication.

A few years ago I was reading an interesting book called *The Social Animal* by David Brooks,[1] and some members of my book club said, "That's great but have you read the one by Carol Tavris and Elliot Aronson called *Mistakes Were Made (but not by me)*?" I picked up a copy and read it three times. Tavris and Aronson explain so simply, so elegantly, why a person can discard your point and adopt a counter position, almost regardless of what you say. I began to understand that some people are not listening because of a whole set of reasons I had not previously considered.

I contacted Carol Tavris to see if she would be willing to talk about climate change denial and the psychology behind our current environmental conflicts. She agreed. She is a very take-charge person, and I was amused when she started the interview herself by asking the first question.[3]

"I assume you want to know why many people aren't receptive to the message of global warming, right? It's the latest version of a question that has puzzled me my whole life: Why is it when you say to somebody: 'Here's some really wonderful evidence that explains ever so clearly why you're wrong,' the person doesn't say, 'Oh thank you, Carol. I've been really waiting for this evidence. I'm just so appreciative.'?"

Scientists are used to changing their thinking, are constantly putting their ideas to the test, risking being shown their hypothesis is wrong. But *cognitive dissonance* is uncomfortable for most people. Tavris defines this as "a state of tension that occurs whenever a person holds two cognitions (ideas, attitudes, beliefs, opinions) that are psychologically inconsistent," such as "smoking can kill me, but I smoke two packs a day." The smoker can reduce the dissonance in one of two ways: either quit smoking or justify smoking by denying or minimizing the evidence that it's harmful. The mechanism of cognitive dissonance keeps us committed to our beliefs—especially beliefs that we have acknowledged publicly, that we have a commitment to or that we have invested time, effort and money into maintaining. This discord produces mental discomfort, which people seek to reduce in ingenious and self-deluding ways.

And so the answer to Carol Tavris's question is twofold. One relates to social psychology (the study of a person in his or her social context, what's happening in their world), and the other relates to what's going on inside that person. Fundamentally, people are resistant to climate change data because of the human resistance to changing our mind, the psychological response to fear messages—especially fear messages we can't do anything about—and the inherent biases in human perception. These are biases that make us seek and

> **The brain is designed with blind spots,**
> **optical and psychological, and one of its**
> **cleverest tricks is to confer on us the comforting**
> **delusion that we, personally, do not have any.**
> **In a sense, dissonance theory is a theory of**
> **blind spots—of how and why people**
> **unintentionally blind themselves so that**
> **they fail to notice vital events and information**
> **that might make them question their behavior**
> **or their convictions.**

CAROL TAVRIS *and* **ELLIOT ARONSON**

remember information that confirms what we believe—and reject, distort or forget information that dis-confirms what we believe.

But another set of factors has to do with the economy and ide-ology. Tavris recalled a time many years ago when she was a young editor at *Psychology Today*, reviewing a book on the Japanese town of Minamata, where people had been severely harmed by industrial pollution. She was struck by the fact these people decided to stay there because that's where their jobs, their homes and their liveli-hoods were. Even though they knew their own children could be deformed, they would not leave. "On a global scale, this is what we see everywhere. In the aftermath of Hurricane Sandy, you would think the logical reasoning would be, 'Let's not rebuild here. We're losing our shoreline; let's build further inland.'" But no, people resist change and want to stay in their community.

She said enormous economic and ideological forces reinforce this tendency when it comes to climate change. "People don't want to acknowledge the danger to the world because of the economic consequences to their work, to their families, to their ways of life. That's a huge and realistic concern." Furthermore, those who have made enormous financial investments in doing things a certain way are unlikely to say: "Right. We'll just take a tremendous loss, close up shop and move into some other business." When you have a combination of economic, ideological and psychological biases all in play, it's very difficult for human beings to easily accept large-scale social and economic change.

I told her that when I did my book tour for *Climate Cover-Up*, not once did I have a climate change denier say, "Okay. You caught me. I was wrong. I admit it. I've changed my mind." The psychologist smiled and said that before we make a decision about anything—"Do I believe in climate change? Do I want to buy a Prius?"—we are at our most open-minded, and we will look for information supporting both choices. But the minute we make a decision, we begin to see all the reasons that were right about it. "We start to overlook and forget any information that suggests we were wrong." Self-justification protects us from the uncomfortable feeling of cognitive dissonance that comes from recognizing we made a mistake; the longer we hold fast to that original decision, the harder it is to change our minds.

In *Mistakes Were Made*, Tavris and Aronson use an image they call *the pyramid of choice.* "Two young men who are identical in terms of attitudes, abilities and psychological health are standing at the top of a pyramid." They are pals and they are undecided about some issue—cheat or don't cheat in an exam, buy this car or that, take drug company money for their research or not. Now one of them makes a decision in one direction, and the other makes a decision in the opposite direction. The minute they do that, they both start looking for evidence to confirm the wisdom of their choices. As they justify their decisions and their beliefs, they each begin moving farther and farther away from each other until, over time, they are standing at the bottom of the same pyramid, miles apart, and they might have come to dislike or even despise each other.

This image can describe most important decisions involving moral choices or life options, Tavris explained. By the time these two former buddies have slid to the bottom, their ambivalence will have morphed into certainty. The two will think they have always felt this way because self-justification works to keep our beliefs consonant with our behavior and our commitments. What's worrying is that their original decision may have been spontaneous, impulsive, perhaps not very well thought out—but every step they take afterward, sets them on a path that they must increasingly justify.

Over time, the more time, effort, money and public face we attach to any of our decisions, the harder it is to climb back up that pyramid and say, "You know what? Gee, halfway down I really should've changed my mind." This is called *the justification of effort phenomenon.* It is very powerful. "We make an early, apparently inconsequential decision, and by justifying it, we start a process of entrapment that increases the intensity of our commitment," Tavris told me. Justification of effort explains why people who invest in a project that tanks will generally find a way to defend that mistake rather than face the alternative, which is to say: "I'm a good, smart, decent person—and I just did something stupid, unethical or incompetent."

Tavris further explained that cognitive dissonance—that state of having two conflicting cognitions or beliefs that clash with each other—is as uncomfortable as being very hungry or thirsty. The mind is highly motivated to reduce that discomfort: "Dissonance is especially painful when the conflict arises between my view of myself and information that disputes that view.

"Most people think of themselves as being better than average," Tavris said with a smile. "We think we're smarter than average, more attractive than average, more competent, more ethical, and so on. (It's very funny: 88 percent of all Americans think they're better drivers than average.) That's good for self-esteem, but actually people with the highest self-esteem have the most trouble accepting the evidence that they made a wrong decision, did something harmful or are holding an outdated belief."

As I listened to her, I realized this is why advocates in any field of conflict have to be careful not to make their opponents more entrenched in their opposition. This is why it's so important to delve into this modern research, to understand these psychological underpinnings of inaction and denial cycles.

Tavris concluded: "The greatest danger we face on the planet is not only from bad people doing corrupt, evil and bad things, but also from good people who justify the bad, evil and corrupt things they do in order to preserve their belief that they're good, kind, ethical people." This is why it's so hard for physicians to hear they need to correct medical errors in hospitals, or prosecutors need to help release those who've been wrongly convicted—in other words, to correct wildly significant errors in their professions.

In *Mistakes Were Made*, Tavris and Aronson noted that self-justification is more dangerous and powerful than intentionally lying to others because it allows people to convince themselves that what they did was right. The thought process often goes something like this: "There was nothing else I could have done.... Actually it was a brilliant solution.... I was doing the best for the nation.... I'm entitled."

This self-talk minimizes our mistakes and poor decisions and interferes with our ability to self-correct. Everyone knows when they are lying, making excuses, finessing their income tax, doing something illegal or immoral. They may consciously lie to avoid being punished, "to duck the fury of a lover," to avoid being sued or sent to prison. But self-justification is completely different and more pervasive, because it allows us to lie to ourselves. It is a self-protective, unconscious mechanism that allows us to keep our self-image intact. Tavris said the feeling of dissonance is sharpest when we have to resolve a conflict between evidence and some important aspect of our self-concept. "You can criticize me for something that isn't part of my self-concept, but criticize something I try to do well and it will really sting. That's the sting we have to pay attention to because that sting is the sign of dissonance."

Cognitive dissonance and justification of effort play a role in politics too. If a member of your party does something stupid or corrupt, you tend to minimize it, but when someone from the opposing party does exactly the same, you'll say, "That's typical of those bastards." One example was Newt Gingrich criticizing Bill Clinton for having an affair in the Oval Office while he himself was having an affair with one of his own interns. Gingrich's ability to blame Clinton, while excusing himself, shows how far people will go to reduce their own cognitive dissonance.

There is no point hectoring people or telling them they are wrong, Tavris and Aronson explained in *Mistakes Were Made*. Anyone who understands dissonance knows that shouting, "What were you thinking?" will backfire, because it translates as, "Boy, are you stupid." Accusations like this cause already embarrassed victims to clam up, withdraw and refuse to talk about what they are doing. "What was I thinking? I thought I was doing the right thing." People need to feel respected and supported, not criticized. This is the inherent risk of advocacy, because if you accuse someone of being stupid, or make them feel foolish or dim, it only serves to reinforce their default position—which is to activate their self-justification.

How does this insight help us in our environmental conflict discussion? What are the factors that cause somebody to jump off the pyramid at the very top, and take a position on a problem? And perhaps more importantly, what do we do when we have two polarized camps at the bottom, both justifying the choices they made?

During my interview with her, Carol Tavris stressed again that there are two things to be concerned about: factors that cause us to come to a belief in the first place and factors causing us to maintain that position. "In all social movements, you are not only justifying the beliefs you've acquired, but you become part of a group of like-minded people, all echoing the reasons you're right."

To understand resistance to information about climate data, we can look at the history of seat belts, smoking or environmental protection laws that were once thought impossible to enact. Revolutionizing people's smoking habits required more than changing people's belief that smoking could kill you. Everyone knew someone who lived to be 93 and smoked every day. To change people's habits we had to apply peer pressure, change laws, change taxes, change social norms and force people onto the street if they wanted to light up.

From Tavris's perspective, you don't transform societies through a change of heart alone; you have to first change the laws, change public notions of what is acceptable or unacceptable behavior and change the economic consequences of the practices you want to alter. "When that happens at a national or systemic level, people's attitudes begin to change." Going back to her image of the pyramid, the goal is to help people form opinions at the top of the pyramid (for the first time); or, when people have dug in their heels, find out what it would take to get them to alter their minds.

I suggested that people likely don't spend a lot of time at the peak of the pyramid, and Tavris agreed. Most have strong beliefs and have already slid down the pyramid, one way or the other, on environmental issues. So the stronger power of persuasion may lie in getting people who believe in social justice and protecting the environment to become more actively involved in changing government regulations and citizen passivity.

Tavris said one of the most important findings in social psychology is that when you just give people a frightening message—"If you have sex, you'll get AIDS. If you smoke, you'll die"—people tune out. But if the scary message comes with something you can do to avert the disaster, such as "Condoms will keep you from getting AIDS," then people are more likely to listen. "One of the great problems with climate change arguments is that we have been made to feel helpless; the problem is overwhelming. 'I could get a gas-efficient car but every time I fly to England, that's the equivalent of, what, how many thousands of miles that I've driven in my car?'" One of the best ways to help people change their behavior is to give them feedback, show them how much money or water they have saved, by practicing methods of conservation.

Tell them it's working and give them hope. Hope is the narrative of freedom and change. It is the great motivator. "Otherwise, let's just dance on the cliff until we fall off. Social reformers and activists are all acting with hope. What keeps us going is seeing how much change has occurred in the past as a model for the kind of change that can occur in the future."

I asked if activists often make things worse by stimulating people's self-justification response. Tavris believes we need two kinds of activists: both extremists and persuaders. "Shell Oil is not going to listen to reasoned persuasion and say, 'Oh, thank you so much for providing us with this information about how we're spoiling the environment. We hadn't realized that.' Nor are the big pharmaceutical companies going to say, 'Oh, thank you for the data showing our drug has actually been killing far too many people.'" These companies want to hide and suppress data, she said. So one tactic of more extreme opponents has been to go after the worst offenders and polluters. They're not going do the right thing until they're forced to, until there are regulations and penalties, and enough consumer protests to warrant making changes.

But change also happens through persuasion, when the public becomes more aware of the kinds of harm these companies are doing. The danger for the accuser, however, arises when they put on the mantle of the do-gooder, the valiant David taking on Goliath. "All of us need to keep reassessing our beliefs, our goals and our methods because we too can be vulnerable to justifying our methods and our beliefs without stopping to ask ourselves if this is the most effective thing we can be doing."

It's not easy for any of us to ask those questions, and Tavris illustrated her point with a personal example of her own dissonance. She used to be opposed to hormone replacement therapy, which she felt was unnecessary, possibly dangerous and most likely another effort by the pharmaceutical industry to sell more drugs than necessary. But when she and a colleague, an oncologist who has studied the issue for many years, looked at the evidence that has accrued over decades, they found that for most women HRT is actually beneficial in prolonging life and quality of life. "That was a big dissonance-inducing discovery for me as I am a big critic of Big Pharma and opposed to taking just about anything. So I know how uncomfortable it feels when you are forced to say, 'Here's something I believed for many years, and I'm wrong.'"

Self-righteousness is a barrier to self-change, and an impediment to persuading others. We don't relish listening to a moralizer or proselytizer trying to persuade us of something without recognizing where we are coming from and what our needs are. Tavris said it is important to have passionate beliefs because they help motivate us to improve the world, but the key is, "to hold those beliefs lightly so that if evidence comes along suggesting we might be wrong, we can give them up without feeling like we are idiots."

She said an ideal way to live with dissonance is by understanding that we can both see ourselves as good people and admit to doing something wrong. We can admit a mistake and seek ways to rectify it in the future. Cognitive dissonance is a blind spot that enhances our pride and activates our prejudices, she and Aronson wrote in their book. When we spoke, Tavris urged us all to watch out for blind spots (just as good drivers do) and to watch ourselves for any signs of post-decision dissonance. We can all stay aware and open-minded by asking ourselves, at certain intervals, "I made this decision or I came to this belief three years ago, is it still the right one? What do people with different points of view have to tell me about this now?"

And be aware of *naïve realism*, the built-in bias that we are not biased. Naïve realism allows people on two sides of any issue, whether it's the Middle East or climate change, to each think their view is the only reasonable one. Social psychologist Lee Ross gave a sample group of Palestinians a peace proposal designed by the Palestinians, but he labeled it as coming from Israelis. He also gave Israelis a peace proposal that had come from Israelis, but was labeled as a Palestinian proposal. Each side soundly rejected the proposals.[4] "They weren't rejecting the idea in the proposal; they were rejecting who they thought it came from."

One way out of this built-in trap, Carol Tavris explained, is to do our best to hear and repeat the opposite camp's point of view. For those of us trying to get more people concerned about climate change, we need to be able to hear deniers' arguments if we are to persuade them to hear ours. Listen openly, and see if you can understand the sources of people's fears and concerns. And then don't ask them to repeat their views—see if you can repeat theirs.

4

Morality Binds and Blinds

with JONATHAN HAIDT

As the themes in this book began to crystalize, I arranged an interview with social psychologist Jonathan Haidt. Haidt, who is a professor of ethical leadership at New York University's Stern School of Business, looks at how ingrained, tribal behaviors can bind and blind us, and shut down open-minded thinking. Looking at the dynamic of polarization from the point of view of tribes and teams is enlightening and useful in this discussion.

Many of those who read my last book, *Climate Cover-Up*, have asked me why people try to discredit scientists, confuse the public and deny climate science. What motivates this kind of activity? How can these paid lobbyists and bogus experts sleep at night? I used to say it was because of money, but I no longer believe it's that simple. The strength and doggedness of these campaigns calls for a deeper look, and Haidt is an expert in the morality and anatomy of persistent beliefs that fly in the face of evidence.

During our interview in New York,[1] the professor explained that human beings are tribal, oriented from birth to band together into groups and teams. And while there is much good to be said for this age-old drive, it is also a potentially dangerous trait that binds and blinds us. Banding together can lead to unreasonable behavior, disagreements and violent conflict because we are not driven by rationality, facts or compelling arguments. Haidt and his colleagues' studies have found that banding together causes some groups of people to pull apart from other groups, to not only go to war but to become polarized along distinct lines, whether it's over gun control or oil sands.[2] Division can be dangerous because when people share values and morals they become part of a team, "and once they engage in the psychology of a team, open-minded thinking shuts down."

Haidt calls this perilous trap *the moral matrix*. And just like in the movie, *The Matrix*, we all have a choice: "You can either take the blue pill and stick to your comforting delusions, or the red pill, learn some moral psychology and step outside the moral matrix," Haidt explained.

Based on research into what Haidt calls the psychological foundations of morality, he explained that an awareness of our moral roots can help us learn to become more civil, more open-minded, to glean a deeper appreciation of the world around us and to balance the yin-yang effect of opposing forces. We come to understand how we can get stuck in a moral matrix and more importantly, how to escape it. "Our righteous minds have been designed by evolution to unite us into teams and divide us against other teams, to blind us to the truth," but if we can step outside our moral matrix we can find balance and truer understanding of each other.

I first learned about Haidt's work while watching his 2008 TED talk, entitled The Moral Roots of Liberals and Conservatives,[3] and later I read his book *The Righteous Mind*, which explains how and why good people become divided by politics and religion.[4]

Haidt began his TED talk by declaring that the worst idea in all of psychology is that the mind is a blank slate at birth. Far from it, he stressed. Children come into the world neurally preprogrammed to easily learn certain things and have difficulty learning others. Brain scientist Gary Marcus said the initial organization of the brain does not rely heavily on experience. "Nature provides a first draft, which experience then revises."[5]

So the question for Haidt is, "what is written in that first draft of the moral mind?" Haidt and his colleagues researched this concept

> **If you want the truth to stand clear**
> **before you, never be for or against.**
> **The struggle between "for" and "against"**
> **is the mind's worst disease.**
>
> SENGCAN[6]

across cultures and even species and came up with a theory that identifies six moral foundations common to all.[7] They are care/harm, fairness/cheating, liberty/oppression, loyalty/betrayal, authority/subversion and sanctity/degradation. Loyalty/betrayal, for instance, relates to patriotism and self-sacrifice, which is why human groups so easily unite to fight other groups. This trait likely evolved from a long history of intertribal struggle, and when we don't have tribes to fight we create sports instead, so our teams can compete in other arenas. "The aspect of purity/sanctity, on the other hand, is an ideology that tells a person they can attain virtue by controlling their body and what they put in it. This is seen in our liberal moralized attitude about food. Purity's not just about suppressing female sexuality."

Haidt said we come into the world pre-wired, organized in advance by these six sources of intuition and emotion that enable us to quickly bond with others, feel compassion, found religions or defend ourselves. This "first draft" is revised and tuned by life experience and culture, just as audio equalizers in a complex sound system regulate sound waves—but the basic human moral matrix remains. Haidt's research has shown that liberals celebrate diversity, are more open to new experiences, crave novelty, question authority and speak for the weak and oppressed, even at the risk of chaos. Conservatives speak for order. They like things that are familiar, safe and dependable, which is why they support institutions and traditions.

Haidt believes it is important to acknowledge and cherish both points of view because they bring balance. Once you accept that liberals and conservatives each have something of value to contribute, the way is open to step outside the moral matrix. "Yin and Yang aren't enemies. Like night and day, both are essential. In the Hindu faith, both Vishnu and Shiva, the preserver and destroyer gods, share the same body." When diversity is understood and valued, we can step out of a battle between good and evil and "use every tool in the toolbox" to create cooperative groups. "Use that passionate commitment to the truth to create a better future for us all."

I asked Haidt about partisan polarization, and he explained that it has increased in the US since the 1980s, and especially in the past 10 years, partly because the two parties have become "purified." If you go back to the 1960s and 1970s, and even into the 1980s, there were liberal Republicans and conservative Democrats, but there is no longer any middle ground. The parties are perfectly distinct, not just in moral visions but in personality, Haidt observed. As the polarizing current becomes more and more powerful, and increasing amounts of money are spent to influence policy, anything with even the "slightest valence" (meaning emotional charge) gets pulled to one side or the other.

Haidt explained that climate change was not always a strictly Leftist issue. There used to be some agreement that it was a serious problem, and both Left and Right "were trending in the same direction until around 2006." But once the Left made it more of a partisan issue and Al Gore made his documentary[8] calling attention to it as a huge problem, the dynamics of politics took over. Difficulties grew when supporters were not just pro-environment but also explicitly anti-industry. Some people in the environmental movement hate industry, hate capitalism and hate corporations. The polarizing current drew the issue strongly to the Left. The Right got pulled in the opposite direction and eventually "got off the bus."

Republicans and Democrats have long demonstrated this binding and blinding behavior. Haidt said Democrats went through "their crazy moralistic period in the 1970s and into the 1980s with identity politics. They favored a whole bunch of policies that were obviously unfair, really offensive to most Americans—about racial preferences, busing, all sorts of things." The Left was in deep denial of science about race and gender at that time. Denial of science is not exclusive to the Right, Haidt reminded me. Back in 1980 there was more denial of science in the Left than the Right, but Bill Clinton "sort of pulled them back to sanity and the centrist movement." The Left reformed itself, moved away from some of its extreme positions and became more pro-business, which you have to be if you want to govern in the US. Then the Republicans got more extreme in the 1990s, and Congress became a much more partisan institution Haidt explained.

As the Republicans circled more and more around their narrative—their sacred values of free enterprise, the family, the Bible, the flag—they formed into an interesting team of libertarians and social conservatives. They became more moralistic and ready to deny evidence, deny science, to believe the worst about their opponents, to believe the worst about scientists. "So, as global warming evidence was getting stronger in the 1990s and into the 2000s, they became more and more extreme, more ready to jump off the cliff."

Haidt said money for advertising campaigns is another factor that plays into growing polarization. Public relations machines are incredibly powerful, devious and manipulative; a confluence of factors around 2005 and 2006 made people congeal around the idea that climate change was a fraud. Haidt told me he once heard American radio host and commentator Glenn Beck say, "Climate change is not about the environment; it's about control." Americans don't like to be told what to do. They don't like the nanny state, and Haidt believes the Right very skillfully pushed certain moral buttons that sowed profound doubt.

I asked if there is any hope that conservatives can change their minds and start taking environmental problems seriously. He suggested those who want to make this happen should think less about direct methods and more about indirect methods. A general principle of moral psychology is this: intuitions come first and strategic reasoning second. If people don't trust the Left, don't trust the environmental or scientific communities, the electromagnet again grows more powerful. If they see scientists and environmentalists as liberals, they won't trust them. Echoing Carol Tavris's image of the pyramid of choice, Haidt explained that *confirmation bias theory* tells us if you doubt, dislike and distrust something in your heart, you're going to look for evidence that confirms that. We human beings tend to say: "I think proposition X is true. Is there any evidence for it? Yes, I just saw some on Fox News. Okay. It's true." This theory explains why direct attacks are not effective. Results are achieved by draining the passion, changing feelings and opening up space for better reasoning.

Haidt cited the gay marriage movement as a prime example. For many years the Left argued, "How does it hurt your marriage if other people marry? Don't they have a right?" But the rights of gay people to marry did not start to change until more people came to know gay people, and they became just people who happened to be gay. The passion to oppose their rights drained away. "Twenty years ago, to be homosexual was laughable, disgusting and strange—but now everybody knows gay people," so gay marriage is losing its emotional charge.

Similarly, Haidt suggested that as climate change advocates focus on issues such as fuel efficiency standards, better light bulbs and ways to make us all less energy dependent, the negative charge will weaken. "If you begin to associate combating climate change with the Apollo program and a gigantic national effort to find technologies that will wean us off the carbon-heavy fuel sources, then it won't seem threatening anymore." Suddenly people will trust the scientists. Change the feelings, and then evidence has a chance.

Polarization is extremely predictable, Haidt explained, and part of the blindness involves perceiving issues increasingly as threats. The more you make something central to your team's mission, the more blind you become, which causes the other side to become blind to your issue. For example, in the US now, more than 50 percent of kids will not live with their two biological parents throughout their childhood, either because of divorce or non-marital childbearing.[9] It's a concern to many, "but people on the Left are unwilling to say marriage is good or necessary because they don't want to risk offending feminists, African-Americans and gay people. So the Left is effectively blind around the issue. If you hitch your environmentalism to a polarizing issue, you can pretty much guarantee that you're painting it with a cloak of invisibility, and the other side is simply not going to see your concern."

Haidt paraphrased a quote by Jesus: "Why do you complain about the speck in your neighbor's eye when you cannot see the plank in your own?"[10] In general, our social cognitive abilities are extremely accurate in our perception of others, but extremely inaccurate in our perception of ourselves.

He added that although it's very difficult to remove people's biases, when in conflict with a person or group, an incredibly valuable tool is to acknowledge where others are right, because in almost any conflict each side is right about something. "If you're Shell Oil you could start by saying: 'Environmentalist, we understand that you're concerned. The oil and gas industry has done some bad things. We've had some major screw ups; we have killed seabirds.' The Left could say to Shell Oil: 'You're not crazy to worship markets. Markets really are amazing things.'"

This is true acknowledgment, the power of empathy, and it lies at the heart of Haidt's message. If our goal is to seek a deeper understanding of the world around us and clear the public square, we must move from self-righteousness to moral humility. It's all about shifting the tone and not being accusatory because, as Haidt explains, each of us has a thin-skinned moral matrix that is the source of our most sacred beliefs.

5

Why We Want To Be Misled

with DAN KAHAN

ONE OF THE FIRST interviews I did for this book was with Dan Kahan at Yale Law School. Yale Law has an interdisciplinary faculty where professors and scholars specialize in everything from economics to psychiatry. Kahan's primary research interests are risk perception, science communication and the application of decision science to law and policymaking. I had come to interview him after reading about his work on the Cultural Cognition Project, which features a team of interdisciplinary scholars who study how cultural values shape people's beliefs and perceptions of risk. I wanted to learn how group values impact risk perceptions and how our interpretation of scientific evidence is shaped by our cultural affiliations.

Cultural cognition describes the tendency of individuals to conform their beliefs about disputed matters of fact—whether relating to global warming as a serious threat or the death penalty as a deterrent to commiting murder—to values that define their cultural identities. Kahan and his colleagues employ social psychology, anthropology, communications theory and political science to chart the impact of this phenomenon and identify its operating mechanisms. In a study published in 2010, Kahan and his colleagues looked at why some members of the public disagree—"sharply and persistently"— about facts on which expert scientists generally agree. The study confirmed that cultural cognition does indeed shape individual beliefs about the existence of scientific consensus, whether about climate change or the disposal of nuclear waste.[1]

My interview with Dan Kahan took place in his office over the course of two hours—time I now affectionately refer to as "My Class at Yale Law."[2] What began as an interview about the impact of corporate misinformation on public denial of climate change became a fascinating lesson in how the public forms opinions about risk and science. It reconfirmed in my mind how futile public arguments involving facts and evidence can be, and deepened my view about how industry misinformation creates confusion. I went into the interview well versed in how people are misled by misinformation and propaganda, but I wanted to learn more about how we mislead ourselves—and about the complicated process of how corrupted cultural networks affect our understanding and our judgments.

While misinformation campaigns certainly play a role in public confusion, Kahan argued that there are more powerful forces at work and that more accurate information will not fix what he calls a *social pathology* that leads to underestimating or denying climate change risk. Nor is the pathology of climate change denial as simple as one group agreeing with real climate scientists and another aligning themselves with charlatans.

Kahan said there is a reason why people allow themselves to be misled and are predisposed to being misinformed. He described two primary influences that play into this vulnerability: confirmation bias and motivated reasoning. *Confirmation bias* is a type of selective thinking in which a person tends to notice and look for what confirms their beliefs, while prompting them to ignore or not favor information that contradicts those beliefs. He described *motivated reasoning* as, "the unconscious tendency of individuals to process information in a manner that suits some end or goal extrinsic to the formation of accurate beliefs." Motivated reasoning is a unifying theme or general class of mechanisms that makes people resist information that threatens their identity.

**People will find the person whose values
they think are more like theirs to be more credible.
And that's how they figure out what to believe,
because they trust people like them.**

DAN KAHAN

These influences propel people to confirm what they already believe and ignore any data to the contrary. These forces can also drive them to develop elaborate rationalizations to justify those beliefs, even if false, and even if logic and evidence point in another direction.

In a paper titled "Motivated Numeracy and Enlightened Self-Government," Kahan studied subjects who were presented with a difficult problem that called upon their ability to draw valid "causal inferences from empirical data."[3] Subjects with high scores in numeracy (the ability to use quantitative information) did much better than others in the group when asked to interpret data about a new skin rash treatment. But interestingly, the subjects' responses were more politically polarized and less accurate when they looked at results from a gun control ban study. In fact, the polarization increased in high numeracy subjects who used their greater reasoning capacity to make sure their interpretation conformed to their politics.

Kahan referred to another paper that showed that when two experts argue about something, even if the issue is remote from the values of those involved, "people will find the person whose values they think are more like theirs to be more credible. And that's how they figure out what to believe, because they trust people like them[-selves]."[4]

Kahan stressed human beings are "really good" at figuring out who to believe about what. This is a critical skill since no one human being could possibly reproduce all the world's knowledge alone. Every scientist builds on previous researchers' work; this is why Sir Isaac Newton said he was standing on the shoulders of giants.

Kahan illustrated this point further by saying he hasn't been to the North Pole himself and even if he had, he wouldn't know how to measure whether the ice was melting. "If you gave me the measuring equipment and I got readings out of it, I wouldn't know what they meant." Kahan explained that we make the sensible decision to go with people who certify for us, in a reliable way, what's true.

We all rely on such trust networks or systems of certification and communication to make the right choices, but sadly these systems sometimes end up being distorted and corrupted. "We wouldn't have the problems we have today if there wasn't the kind of concentrated, orchestrated effort to try to cause division.... Just as we can pollute the natural environment, we can pollute public discourse."

Public controversy over climate change is often attributed to or-dinary citizens' limited knowledge of science, their poor reasoning capacity or assumed inability to assess technical information. But a study conducted by the Cultural Cognition Project and published in the journal *Nature Climate Change* found no support for this at all. "On the whole, the most scientifically literate and numerate subjects were slightly less likely to see climate change as a serious threat," reported Kahan. Those with the greatest science literacy and capacity for technical reasoning were, in fact, among the most polar-ized.[5] Kahan theorized that this discrepancy arises from a conflict between belief systems—a conflict between *individuals* who form beliefs in line with those held by others with whom they share close ties and the *collective* in which everyone shares in making use of the best available science to promote common welfare.

I asked Kahan, "Isn't the whole idea behind critical thinking that you try not to let your beliefs get in the way of facts and evidence?"

Yes, he said, but belief is not a function of will. You don't choose what you believe; you believe what you believe because you are furnished with the kinds of evidence that impel a certain kind of cognition. People have what Kahan called a "commonwealth" of sensibilities, values and dilemmas that exert control over them and can cause them to misunderstand things. We all rely on people who confirm what we think and on systems of certification, but because our beliefs are connected to who we are and our personal history, they are sometimes distorted.

The Cultural Cognition of Scientific Consensus study showed that when people get new information they can update prior beliefs. This happens, however, only if they recognize the new information as valid. He explained: if you put people in a room and give them a really hard math problem, 90 percent of them won't know the answer. What typically happens is that the people who are ignorant of math will converge on the 10 percent who have that knowledge, not because that group tells them how to do the math problem, but because the 90 percent know something—how to identify others who know what they're talking about.[6]

The process hinges on trust networks and the human skill of being able to find the right kinds of affiliations, so each person can plug into "different networks of certification." That's the normal science communication organism working: You don't have to be an expert in medicine to be adept at choosing a competent doctor.

But Kahan pointed out that something is happening in current discourse to cause systems of certification to be less reliable than usual, to corrupt trust networks. Sometimes it is because people are manipulated, "and there are some fringe groups out there that say, 'Screw Science!'" But Kahan believes there are two more significant, reciprocal elements at work: "One is the orchestrated and deliberate attempt to misinform, and the other is a kind of vulnerability and disposition to being misled." How far you can get with the former depends in large part on the latter.

Dan Kahan believes we need to improve the science of science communication so we can transmit knowledge accurately, especially now, because people are not paying attention to debates about science. Also, there is a science of how to mislead people about science, and there are plenty of people who have a big interest in fueling division. They are not playing a constructive role because they may have vested interests or are mired in "the error of zealotry."

When I asked Kahan how we can move toward healthy dialogue and agreement, he said an effective way to strike communication gold is to start mining better narrative resources.

"We know from cognitive psychology that people process information in narratives." When there is a good guy and a bad guy; some kind of recognizable drama; a beginning, middle and end; as well as a moral and a conclusion, people resonate with the story and make sense of what you are saying. Culturally diverse people are motivated by different kinds of narratives, characters and dramas, so we need an inventory of narratives to convey information across different groups.

He also stressed there is also a narrator in every story, a speaker somewhere, and an audience will be very attentive to that; this is another influence that should affirm identity and not threaten it. Pluralistic advocacy needs to think about the message and the messenger, about the right narrative and the right spokesperson to deliver it, across myriad groups. When all these align, each person is able to converge on truth in their own way. A pluralistic advocacy environment is one where, "people can see people like them on both sides of the issues, and also people who are not like them on both sides." The goal is to find a narrative that people relate to and embed a message that will lead to open-minded consideration.

Kahan explained that we must converge on the truth and respond to problems by respecting each other and letting go of intolerance. "It's not healthy to be imperialistic about one's own story and meanings." We need to acknowledge that other people have different sets of values, and we need to give up our compulsion to be right. That is zealotry. "We are thinking human beings and we're opinionated, and there is going to be a plurality of different kinds of ways people think...We should agree that that's something we're going to promote."

A Failure
To Communicate

6

Facts Are Not Enough

with GEORGE LAKOFF

I FIRST BEGAN READING the works of linguist and cognitive scientist George Lakoff about 15 years ago and was struck by the Berkeley professor's now famous ideas about what he calls frames. In public relations our stock in trade is messaging, because our role is to create understanding with maximum clarity and brevity. We work in the world of sound bites and elevator pitches that are designed to be short and pithy, and we rarely have the time or budget to delve into frames or deeply moving narratives.

I wanted to better understand the difference between messages and frames, to know how frames work and how to manage them and to understand how frames impact facts and scientific evidence in public discourse, or when shaping opinion.

When we met,[1] Lakoff described *frames* as metaphors and conceptual frameworks that we use to interpret and understand the world. They give meaning to the words we hear more than the other way around, because words don't have objective meanings independent of these metaphors. Frames are structures of thought that we all use every day to determine meaning in our lives; frames govern how we act. They are ultimately a blend of feelings, values and data related to how we see the world.

We can't think without frames, Lakoff explained. "Every thought you have, every word is defined in terms of a frame. You can't say any word that's meaningful without it activating a frame." Frames permeate everything we think and say, so the people who control language and set its frames have an inordinate amount of power.

Lakoff explained that if you do a bad job of framing your story, someone else will likely do it for you and his comments reminded me of something my mentor in the PR business, Mike Sullivan, once said: "If you don't tell them, someone else will—and it will be bad." What Mike meant was if you are an unwilling or ineffective communicator, you leave yourself wide open to someone else doing serious damage.

A frame is a way of looking at the world that is value laden, and like a metaphor it conjures up all kinds of thoughts and emotions. Jackie Kennedy used a frame when she referred to her life as Camelot. "Ethical oil" and "tax relief" are also frames. Such words evoke subconscious images and meanings, as opposed to factual statements such as "10 million scallops are dead," a headline that appeared in February 2014 in a Vancouver Island newspaper.[2]

What came to be called Climategate was an international campaign to discredit scientists on both sides of the Atlantic just before the 2009 Copenhagen summit on climate change. It took the momentum to set targets out of the conference. I was astonished to see how a group of legitimate climate scientists, with stacks of peer-reviewed evidence on their side, could lose debates to a group of people who had none—all because of a lens created by mischief-makers. Climategate was a battle of frames versus facts, and the frames won.[3]

The truth is, facts alone don't change minds, said Lakoff, who wrote a book called *Don't Think of an Elephant*, which explains how to frame political debates in terms of values not facts.

Lakoff believes that the progressive community contributes to confusion in the public square because of an outdated understanding of reason and consequent lack of persuasive communication. During our interview, he told me that progressives need a mental model that goes beyond cold, logical messaging that's directly correlated

**Get clear on your values,
and start using the language of values.
Drop the language of policy.**

GEORGE LAKOFF

to reality—a model that should embrace metaphors, a marriage of emotion and logic.

Liberals have an unemotional view of reason that dates back to French philosopher Descartes. Lakoff explained that when conservatives want to go into politics they study business, marketing and what makes people tick, whereas progressives study political science, law and public policy. Progressives don't study cognitive science, neurology or how the brain works. "They learn a false view of reason that goes back to the 1600s...that says reason is conscious, logical and unemotional."

It wasn't long ago that risk communications experts, who study the power of facts, also assumed that giving people more information and evidence would ensure they made better decisions. But research shows facts don't change minds, at least not in the way we think they do.

Lakoff explained that cognitive and brain science research has shown that reason is not rational without emotion, without an overlay of values to make sense of facts. Simply put, frames trump facts. "We have thousands of metaphors structuring our brains," Lakoff told me. "We think in terms of them all the time, and they're not random; they're not mythical; they're things that allow us to get around in the world. We have to use them. Words aren't neutral;" they are the structure we use to think.

We should all have a commitment to the truth, he continued, but not let an understanding of facts overwhelm our job, which is to change the brains of people out there. "Every time you argue, you change your brain. Every time you tell somebody something else, you're changing brains, because everything you think is physical; it's all in the circuitry of your brain." But just speaking the truth isn't enough to convince people of new ideas. If facts are to make sense and be perceived as urgent, they must be framed in terms of deep, deep values.

George Lakoff's advice is short and sweet: To be an effective communicator get clear on your values and start using the language of values. Drop the language of policy. "People do not necessarily vote their self-interest. They vote their identity. They vote their values."[4] Lakoff believes so-called inaction and apathy should warn progressives that the conservatives are winning the communications battle between moral imperatives: "It's time to decide—either we are all in this together, or it's every man for himself."

Progressive morality says citizens act responsibly to provide infrastructure, education, health care, transportation and basic research for one another. Progressives constrain stock markets and protect bank accounts. They believe that private profit depends upon public provision. Conservatism is all about personal responsibility. The importance of public services is minimal when compared with the benefits of private enterprise. Conservatives promote stock markets and build banks. They believe that human effort creates wealth.

Of course some people are conservative about some things and progressive about others. Lakoff calls this *bi-conceptualism*; it means you can have both moral systems operating in your brain at the same time, each inhibiting the other from time to time. The more active one is, the stronger it gets, and that's where language and communication come in. It's also why media influences matter so much, as do the ways we communicate.

In politics and social issues, frames are hierarchically structured and at the top of that hierarchy are the moral frames. So the question often is this: Is this a frame where citizens care about each other, act responsibly and where there is a robust sense of what's good for all? Or is the frame telling us that someone believes they have the freedom to access their own self-interest but need not care about the interests of others?

When it comes to environmental issues, Lakoff explained that these conflicting moralities are tied to two very different ideas of our relationship with nature. For progressives, we are a part of nature and dependent on the environment. Nature has inherent value. For conservatives, we are separate from and dominant over nature. Nature's value is determined by its direct utility to people. Lakoff was quick to note that this is a simplification because most people aren't ideologues, and bi-conceptuals are generally open to persuasion in either direction. The moderate has no ideology.

Every word is defined by an individual frame. A frame is a neural circuit. A neural circuit is made up of connections of neurons joined together by synapses. When a circuit is activated the synapses get stronger. If that circuit inhibits another circuit, then that other circuit's synapses get weaker. When the synapses are stronger, it is easier to activate an idea in someone's mind and therefore easier for it to spread to other issues. "So, repetition is what strengthens synapses. And it doesn't matter if it is accurate."

Suppose you're a conservative, he said, and you want to create a frame that fits your moral system, but let's suppose it has nothing to do with truth. You may be saying, for example, that cutting corporate taxes will create jobs. We know that's false. Corporations are making more profits than ever before, are not hiring people because they're outsourcing work, reaping the benefits of cheap labor in other countries or using more technology. They're not "creating jobs." So this is a false statement. But if conservatives call themselves job creators and repeat it over and over, people will think that cutting corporate taxes will create more jobs. The words are like a recurring jingle, stimulating a synapse and creating a thought pattern. That frame is activated over and over, and every time it is reactivated it grows stronger.

I asked Lakoff if it's possible to set the record straight. Every time we say, "Those are not job creators," do we step into the job creator frame and imprint it again? By outlining facts, even in a logical statement of contradiction, do we always help reinforce the other side's point of view?

Yes, he said. You lose the persuasion battle when you consistently step into your opponent's frame; it reinforces their morality and their argument in the minds of your audience. The way to respond. is to not mention the other frame. Only mention yours. Always start with your frame and stay in it. Always be on the offensive; never act defensively.

Framing is a system that has evolved because it works for everyday life, said Lakoff. "Free will is not totally free. It is radically constrained by the frames and metaphors shaping your brain and limiting how you see the world. Those frames and metaphors get there, to a remarkable extent, through repetition in the media."[5]

Everything you have learned is stored physically in your brain, Lakoff stressed. Every frame is in a brain circuit; every metaphor is in a brain circuit; every image is in a brain circuit. Your whole moral system is in your brain. If you hear something that doesn't fit with what's in your brain, it will go in one ear and out the other unless you are the type of person who remembers things that don't quite fit and worries about them. But most people don't.

Progressives must realize that their old-fashioned view of reason is false—that Descartes and the information injection theory of communication have not panned out.

7

Matters of Concern

with BRUNO LATOUR

FRENCH PHILOSOPHER Bruno Latour agrees that facts don't change minds. They don't clear up controversies, and they don't solve problems, especially regarding environmental science communications, where arguments cyclone around facts, confusing the public and getting in the way of action. We need a different approach said Latour,[1] who is a professor at Sciences Po Paris, where he founded and directs a groundbreaking social sciences facility called médialab. It is a high-tech hub for leading-edge research that applies digital tools and technologies to enhance research in the social sciences.

When we met in Paris, Latour told me we should put aside matters of fact and focus instead upon matters of concern, a conclusion he arrived at after having studied everything from environmental crises to atmospheres of democracy. His advice seemed simple enough, but why is this necessary and what does it mean, exactly?

Latour has authored dozens of books including *Laboratory Life*, *Pandora's Hope*, *We Have Never Been Modern*, *Science in Action*, and *The Politics of Nature: How to Bring the Sciences into Democracy*, all of which explore the intersections of science and politics.[2] In 2013 he also won the Holberg Prize for his ambitious analysis and reinterpretation of modernity, which led the committee to state that his work reaches far beyond the "studies of the history of science, art history, history, philosophy, anthropology, geography, theology, literature and law."[3]

In a 2005 essay called "From Realpolitik to Dingpolitik—An Introduction to Making Things Public,"[4] Latour referred to an infamous address given by former US Secretary of State Colin Powell to the United Nations. In this 2003 speech Powell attested to the "unambiguous and undisputable fact of the presence of weapons of mass destruction in Iraq." Of course, it wasn't long before the world realized that this "fact" was groundless, but at the time Powell prefaced his remarks by saying, "My colleagues, every statement I make today is backed up by sources, solid sources. These are not assertions. What we are giving you are facts and conclusions based on solid intelligence."

Never was the difference between facts and assertions more abused than on that day, wrote Latour. "Mr. Powell tried to distinguish the rhetoric of assertions from the undisputable power of facts. He failed miserably. Having no truth, he had no eloquence either. Can we trace again the frail conduits through which truths and proofs are allowed to enter the sphere of politics?"[5]

Latour explained that this question is actually moot because the solution lies not simply in getting facts straight and sorting out truth from the rhetoric once and for all. "Transparent, unmediated, undisputable facts" have become so rare today that to offer a public proof—big enough and certain enough to convince the whole world of the presence of a phenomenon or of a looming danger—seems now almost beyond reach.

And so Latour said it is important now to put facts aside, to abandon the worn-out cliché of incontrovertible so-called truths and to compare assertions instead. With these inferior types of proof we may come to a conclusion at last. He suggested that turning to matters of concern suits the modern era, because we are in a time of huge sea change, of transformations that will encompass our conceptions of science and understanding of objectivity. The enormous complexities of both scientific research and political activity at every level are leading us to a growing appreciation that objects and issues "are much more interesting, variegated, uncertain, complicated, far reaching, heterogeneous, risky..." than we have ever believed.

Even today, people like Powell are accustomed to sweeping away opposition by claiming the superiority of their facts, but Latour explained that, after studying real scientists in action during his 40-year career, he understands that, in the realm of science, facts are always the source of careful scrutiny, inquiry and discussion. Whereas in the realm of politics, matters of fact are too often held to be self-evident weapons to be used to end a debate rather than foster discussion or dialogue.

We talked about the complexity of climate change, and Latour explained that the field involves a vast body of research that encompasses the knowledge and practical work of thousands of scientists, the multi-faceted accomplishments of an immense number of individuals. The problem, he asserted, is not a lack of information or facts. Quite the opposite. Climate science has produced masses of information, but Latour points out, "Knowing is made up of so many different loops and different layers that it takes a lot of time to measure out what we know." He sees a disconnect between what is known—what facts are, what knowledge means and why those facts are significant—precisely because of the time it takes to evaluate data, to discuss and project its implications and to consider how to act on that knowledge. We will never have such good data on climate change as we have today, he stressed, "because now we have put the thing out of whack" (referring to Earth's climate balance).

Latour believes that action on climate change has been stalled because our knowledge has been muddled by political wrangling and because of the daunting demands that climate change action requires "the complete transformation of all the details of existence of seven billion people." It's no easy task to ask the entire world's human population to change their lives completely, and small wonder people respond with an unwillingness to believe we must change. We have all become what Australian public ethics professor Clive Hamilton refers to as climate skeptics because adopting this stance allows us to avoid doing what we should.[6] It's not a question of knowing and not acting—what we are witnessing is global resistance to change.

The transformation we need is on a scale that even the most radical revolutionaries—whether Marx, Lenin or even Stalin—could never have imagined. Their ideas of revolution were superficial compared to the colossal shift now necessary, said Latour, who is actually pleased that climate change has become so controversial, because it drives home the reality of what we are facing, even if people are still unwilling to act.

He noted that some positive advances were made during the past 30 years, when Republicans and Democrats in the US managed to agree on many laws about climate and the environment, but now people have marched farther apart and are more opposed than ever. Such polarization is propelling issues of climate change into the political arena.

This is a realm where we clearly witness the chasm between matters of fact and matters of concern. Latour explained that we used to have an idea that action followed facts, and that those who didn't follow were ignorant or irrational. "Actually, this has never been the case in the whole history of science, but this was our idea, that you settle the facts first and then get into the question of politics and values." Even if this were true, it would not work in the case of climate change because the event is ongoing, having lasted and developed for centuries. "Nothing of that could be put in the normal framework of an action following knowledge."

Because so many people disagree about it, and because climate change is becoming an enormous matter of concern, Latour urges scientists not to stay sequestered in their labs, simply doing their studies and clinging to the idea that they should be disinterested and impartial. Scientists put themselves in a precarious position if they hold fast to a position that they are "just stating the facts" and should not politicize science. At the end of the day, scientists are human beings who have to make a living: They are drawing salaries and competing for grants from government, industry and other institutions. Latour wants them to stand up and fight, with full disclosure, full respect, scrupulous honesty, honoring of the democratic process.

We have long passed the point where we can talk about a fight between good, clean science and science that has been sullied and distorted by personal and public interests. It is time to fight, to get political and "fly under one's own colors;" as the US intellectual Walter Lippmann once said, "It is a fight for the world." Otherwise, Latour said flatly, if world temperatures continue to rise we will be living in a very different place, and that will end the argument. Latour is currently writing a play, and at the end of the debate between his central characters (a scientist and a climate skeptic) the audience is told the scientists are now on the warpath. "I think that's a powerful way of putting it."

We need scientists to become more political because pure evidence—facts, figures and flow charts—cannot form an adequate basis for public debate. Why? Primarily because the public is not equipped to get to the bottom of such a discussion or analyze all these facts. "And having to work within a notion of consensus closes off argument and authority. We become completely mired in all the epistemology of getting the facts straight." We must talk about concerns and interests instead.

So what exactly is the public's role?

One answer lies in what Latour considers to be one of the best books on democratic politics of the 20th century, Walter Lippmann's *The Phantom Public*.[7] In this famous tome Lippmann described the public as being like someone who arrives late, in the second act of a play, glances around the stage, leaves before the performance is over and makes a snap judgment as to who are the bad guys and who are good. And yet despite this "incompetency," as Lippmann called it, members of the public are asked to align themselves with one side or the other whenever they go to the polls. They do this by relying on experts to help them choose their alliances.

I asked Latour how a collective can operate if the experts can't be trusted, if the trust networks are corrupted and people are up to mischief? He said the problem becomes especially acute when the issues at stake are unprecedented—as in the case of climate change—and when there is a dispute in which experts fail to agree. Then it is up to the public "in all its incompetency" to try and align itself with one side or the other. Lippmann, who died in 1974, said we can never expect more from the public, and Latour agreed, saying it has become much worse since Lippmann's day.

If this is the case, what can we do? The only solution is to help the public detect partisanship, said Latour: "Lippmann had this marvelous definition of the role of the intellectual as the one who produced quick detection of partisanship." I was happy to hear that this is why Latour uses our DeSmogBlog in his research. "It is a bias detector," he said, adding that he created his cartography of controversy project because he, too, wants more bias detectors to be available.

At the Sciences Po médialab, Latour created a tool he calls *controversy mapping*, which is now used around the world. It focuses on controversies that swirl around scientific knowledge, rather than homing in on scientific facts or outcomes themselves. Because knowledge of the truth is always complicated, something like controversy mapping can offer insights into the process of producing knowledge, of how something comes to be considered true. Mapping reveals how a view of pure science often ignores important facets and perspectives.

The best thing the public can do is to try and detect partisanship, said Latour, adding this is what he endeavors to do with controversy mapping. Lippmann does not suggest a person can ever achieve a state of complete non-partisanship, but at least we can learn to detect biases faster and more effectively, "by crude and oral signs. That's all you can do."

A key part of the process is learning to decipher who the experts are. Debate is the weapon of the epistemologist. Climate skeptics say they want a fair debate—"and for every climatologist there seems to

**It's not a question of getting the facts straight
and sorting out truth from the rhetoric once and for all....
It's a question of changing the conditions of existence,
not just of a few people, but of seven billion people.**

BRUNO LATOUR

be a climate skeptic"—but Latour advises against participating in any debate about science and facts, because there can be no resolution. This doesn't mean we should back off, be disinterested or neutral, which he likens to taking part in a boxing match with your hands tied behind your back. Instead all parties in a decision-making process need to declare their interest.

The French scholar said if he were mapping climate change, he would totally ignore the critics and individuals who sow mischief. "They would not even appear because they are not publishing scientific papers." These disputes are politically motivated and arise because we are faced with a revolutionary transformation that no one has ever lived through. We need to adjust our philosophy of science to the new situation, so "let's talk about interests instead of disinterest." We may not agree on the interpretation of measurements, and there may be disputes about instruments of calibration, but if we have scientific papers that are peer reviewed, this eliminates the so-called other side.

When uninformed people talk about ineffective climate change models, Latour labels such public misinformation and confusion "science of deliberate ignorance." Deliberately misleading comments were put forth years ago about smoking and have been used to deny the Holocaust during World War II in Europe; Stanford University's Robert Proctor calls this phenomenon culturally induced ignorance or doubt.[8] According to Latour, struggles between rhetoric and science have been waged for 20 centuries, from Socrates to Powell, and everybody uses rhetoric, even scientists. But it need not make any difference—because the real gap is between well-constructed and badly constructed science, not between rhetoric and reason.

However, Latour does worry about the way scientific facts are wielded by environmentalists who deliver dire warnings. These may be well intentioned, but Latour suggested that many ecologists are frightening people with their apocalyptic predictions. "We are talking about seven billion people having to convert to other energy resources, but after seeing films showing a series of catastrophic exponential curves paired with very strong music, the only reasonable consequence is that we do nothing." There is little point in creating a message that leads to paralysis. This is a Fox News attitude and should be fought by all possible means, Latour said.

Another source of pollution in the public sphere comes from an argument about inevitability, says Latour, adding this was Al Gore's position in his film *An Inconvenient Truth*. It is not a wise strategy to define a situation as inevitable or out of our control. "This is a negation of politics—because you don't do politics with inevitability," explained Latour. If you send a message to people that there's no other possibility, that it's too late—the result is inaction. To get people politically interested, Latour suggested that the message must give them the will to find a way out of the dilemma. If you produce a message that removes the will, even if it's a completely informed message, a factual message supported by 200 Nobel Prize winners, the result will be inaction. This is not the situation we want; "science is not about inevitability and ineluctability."

To remedy this situation, Latour suggested that we "abandon the notion of truth," at least the cumbersome perception of truth which either plays the role of an arbiter or gives us solid ground on which to stand together. People assemble, he said, only when there is no arbiter and when they don't yet stand on common ground. People assemble politically because "they share the dispute," because they are concerned about the same issue and need to reach a settlement. He noted there is debate about every single infrastructure topic these days—whether it's oil, windmills or solar panels—not to mention arguments about everything from tuna to whales, from vitamins to meat. This is another source of pollution. We used to believe that experts would deliver a disinterested set of facts, which were then discussed by politicians who made sound decisions based on good information. We, the public, do not believe this anymore.

While he encourages and welcomes the move away from matters of fact toward matters of concern, Bruno Latour stressed it is a dangerous time because we have not learned to navigate these waters yet. He used two examples: In the past, if you were troubled about whether or not to vaccinate your children, you discussed it with your doctor and an epidemiologist. Now there is much more information in the public sphere, and controversy overflows around this and almost every topic. If you want to know whether to support the development of windmills in your area, you will find myriad opinions on the topic. Few experts agree, and they don't just talk about windmills, but about law and the price of electricity.

In the past, revolutionaries sought to change the way people lived, but not in every aspect. Now every detail of the way we live comes under scrutiny. People attack you because you bought cherries in winter, because of your carbon footprint. Every single detail is disputed, and we are made to feel guilty. When we seek advice today, we find disputes by experts who hold different sets of values. In France, for example, there is a fierce controversy being waged in the newspapers, "not in the scientific papers," about genetically modified organisms. "And now we have people privately auditing science—which would not happen in a world where people believed the scientific community. It's completely impossible, completely implausible."

And while he shakes his head at this turn of events, he believes it is healthy to have disputes because they lead to the next step, which is to ask the question, What kind of world do we want to build, and how can we organize a discussion about that without a political institution or forum that has been designed for the purpose?

Latour did not develop his theory of abandoning facts, and setting truth aside, because he believes there is no truth. What he believes is that absolute truth exists only in a laboratory, and truth has many faces in the public sphere. When everybody declares they speak in the name of truth, what do we achieve in public discourse? Nothing. Instead we have *modus vivendi*: We agree to disagree. "Truth distorts the situation, because it is not really a scientific term, and it asks too much from the conversation.

"So let's abandon the notion of truth, not because we don't want objectivity, but because it plays the role of a referee which would be arbiter of our dispute." When there is no arbiter, we need to assemble; where we don't share the common ground, we can share the dispute. If someone comes to the assembly and says, "I have my values, and this value can't be trampled on," or "I have matters of fact and they are indisputable," then no assembly is possible. This is why he believes we are witnessing a civilization shift where we can't use old epistemology on climate change.

Latour explained it is impossible to make a successful argument for climate change "in the straitjacket of normal politics. This is what happened in Copenhagen." They tried to find solutions, but the problem, of course, is that to have an assembly of this shape and magnitude we need to employ the God of Politics as our arbiter.

People could introduce themselves very politely to each other and say, "I am presenting the CO_2 curve with these instruments, and it cost this to produce. I have my own interest as a scientist. I hope to get the Nobel Prize for this beautiful thing here. And now, what is your card? Yes. Ah, you work for the oil industry, and it's perfectly respectable. We need the oil industry. What world do you want to build? And are you representing the penguin? Ah, very good." In other words, full disclosure, full respect between everyone participating in the conversation.

We are in a fight for the Earth, said Latour. This is the big political point that is missing from disputes about the environment: Who is the enemy? Are we the enemy of the Earth, or is she our enemy?

Duped and How

8

The Self-Regulating Psychopath

with JOEL BAKAN *and* NOAM CHOMSKY

AN OVER RELIANCE on facts and a questionable belief in the power of reason contribute to today's toxic conversations and acrimonious dialogue, but another area of great concern is propaganda, a polluting and polarizing behavior that is arguably as vast and destructive as any of the cultural or social forces already discussed. What's more, in the case of modern corporations, deregulation has legitimized the use of unbridled propaganda and created a regulatory, legal and financial system that virtually demands it.

In his book *The Corporation: The Pathological Pursuit of Profit and Power*,[1] author, filmmaker and law professor Joel Bakan traced the corporation's rise to dominance, right back to its origins centuries ago. Balkan illuminated how these juggernauts are required by law to elevate their own interests above those of others and pursue their goals with rampant self-interest, sometimes without regard for moral limits.

After seeing the film Balkan made from his book,[2] I was keen to speak with him. I was interested in his views on the role some corporations play in corrupting public discourse, something I had occasionally seen up close during my career in PR. I asked Bakan what inspired him to write *The Corporation*, and he explained the project was driven by a passion to inform people about an institution that increasingly governs their lives and poisons public discourse.

The law professor sees the contemporary corporation as a "very strange, potentially dangerous and destructive institution."[3] Back in the late 1990s he started to observe the power of corporations as they exploded into public awareness, spearheading the development of globalization, deregulation and privatization. Governments began to abdicate much of their regulatory oversight and free corporations from legal constraints. As a result, corporations emerged as self-governing institutions with the single goal of serving their own interests and those of their shareholders.

Bakan's work does not seek to vilify or analyze the people who run corporations or work for them. He critiques the institutional nature of the corporation as legally created, saying it is an invention that has been imbued with characteristics that, if observed in a human being, would swiftly be diagnosed as psychopathic.

This view initially seemed a little extreme to me, as I built my business around representing successful corporations and never saw anything remotely like this in the companies I worked with. But then Bakan outlined the characteristics of a psychopath: including callous unconcern for the feelings of others; incapacity to maintain enduring relationships; reckless disregard for the safety of others; deceitfulness, repeated lying and cheating people for profit; incapacity to experience guilt; failure to conform to social norms with respect to lawful behavior. Looking at this list in relation to the excesses on Wall Street, the guiles and machinations of big banks, the environmental record of oil and gas companies, the misinformation campaigns we wrote about in *Climate Cover-Up* and the lies and lack of guilt in the tobacco industry, I began to see Bakan's point.

"Not only have we created an institution in the image of a psychopathic human being, but we've actually conferred personhood on it... and as a society we've given it immense power to govern every aspect of our lives," Bakan said. Increasingly, corporations have limited legal obligation to be concerned about the environment but are compelled

The corporation's unbridled self-interest victimizes individuals and society.

JOEL BAKAN

to do what's best for their shareholders, whether that means investing to ensure a favorable scientific environment, favorable public opinion environment or favorable political environment so that they can lower production costs and increase profits.

That's not a conspiracy, Bakan stressed. "That's just the logical dynamic of a particular institution."

Corporations do an excellent job of churning out masses of marketing materials that suggest they are doing the right things, but when you look at the actual record, they are not being responsible to social interest, nor can they be expected to be. "How can you expect a psychopath to be self-regulating? The concept doesn't make any sense," said Bakan, who calls corporate social responsibility an oxymoron.

I found Bakan's analysis more believable than the evil CEO explanation or any conspiracy theory. The current system makes it incredibly difficult for a corporation to behave any differently. These companies run on shares, return of stock options, and their whole structure demands they do nothing to jeopardize profits. It's an oversimplification to turn this fact into a good guy, bad guy narrative because corporations are required by law to act this way.

Bakan noted that some of his best friends work in corporations, and many excellent employees are genuinely committed to social values such as the environment. They want to see their companies doing good things in the world, not causing harm. But when they walk into their offices they are "metaphorically and practically" bound by the institutional demands of their corporations, and that means "social responsibility to stakeholders can only be strategic." Their critical path must be to serve shareholder profits—that's been the unique nature of the institution and its legal obligations since corporations were first formed.

Corporations were first conceived in the late 19th century as immensely powerful tools to attract large sums of capital; they created massive projects such as railroads and more recently airlines and the Internet. They were mighty, effective investment capital vehicles, and they were constrained so they would not cause more harm than good. Beginning in the 1930s "there began to develop a robust regulatory system and regulatory state," Bakan observed, but in the 1980s we began to see a dismantling of regulation, which continues today. "Now the notion is, Let's let the powerful vehicle do its own thing and hope it constrains itself…Somehow everything will trickle down and play out, and the market will take care of it so everything will be fine.[3] Well, everything isn't fine," said Bakan.

Today's corporation, as an institution, lacks any intrinsic or internal ability to constrain itself morally or ethically, and Bakan sees this as very dangerous: "If you put blinders on a donkey, that donkey is going to do a much better job of going straight down the street and pulling the cart. But it will not see what's happening at the sides, and it won't have any responsibility for that."

Over the past 30 years or so, "there has basically been a deal, and the deal is that government would become less involved in demanding that corporations be socially responsible, providing corporations would take on the task of regulating themselves and becoming more socially responsible." It used to be that public laws demanded that corporations toe the line, but now we rely on the private choices of individual companies. Many corporations talk the talk of social and environmental responsibility, but Bakan sees a huge gap between words and action, and said the deal has not been a good one for the people, for the environment or for stakeholders.

Chief Justice Leo E. Strine Jr. of the US State of Delaware has written that corporate sustainability misunderstands Delaware law and that it "is not only hollow but also injurious to social welfare to declare that directors can and should do the right thing by promoting interests other than stockholder interests."[4]

Corporations are invested in creating a scientific domain that is favorable to them and hostile to those who criticize them. For instance, a pharmaceutical company is legally bound to act in ways that serve its shareholders, and it will naturally seek to shape public perception about science, "to control science for its own ends."

Bakan observed that public relations machines have worked hard to repress the true nature of corporations and convey the notion they "are just like you and me...warm and fuzzy, like a good neighbor. They are [the] Michelin Man and Ronald McDonald." Massive amounts of money have been poured into efforts to paint a caring human public face on corporations, to present them as benevolent servants of humanity. "The extent to which this has been successful has been a disaster for democracy and for various values like the environment," Bakan said flatly. A good example of how companies edit information to promote their point of view was an Enbridge Northern Gateway Pipeline's campaign that showed a map that erased about 1,000 square kilometers of islands from the Douglas Channel, in an attempt to make the company's proposed oil tanker route look less treacherous. This campaign also included the slogan, "It's a path to world class safety standards and low environmental impact." In another Enbridge ad, accompanying an emerald-green underwater scene, was a poem that included the lines: "A limitless pool of life/A playground for the tiny and giant things that live within it/And a gateway to the other side."[5] Bakan commented, while corporate social responsibility in some instances does some good, it is most often merely a token gesture that serves to mask the corporation's true purpose.

Bakan stressed that because the corporation as an institution lacks any moral or ethical constraints, it is necessary to impose constraints externally through regulation "and find a balance between what it can do well and the harm it will inevitably cause if not constrained."

I asked Bakan why the public has failed to demand more regulation. "That's the $64,000 question," he said, and it has to do with the manufacture of ideology, with the manufacture of public opinion, with the role that for-profit, advertising-driven media plays in forming public opinion, the lack of critical-thinking training in our education system—and all the various ways in which knowledge is constructed in our society. "We citizens have been asleep at the switch."

Public awareness is seen as a danger by governments and ruling elites, said linguist and cognitive scientist Noam Chomsky, one of this continent's leading political commentators and a professor emeritus at MIT. That's because it can interfere with the primary concern of business, which is the enrichment of the very rich in the short term. Chomsky explained that an oil company executive, for instance, may be personally concerned about greenhouse gases or habitat loss, but in their institutional world they cannot express that worry or step out of their corporate role. "These are very deep problems; they are institutional, not individual."

Chomsky wasted no time telling me exactly what he believes is at the root of the problem: "The government is not our government. It is not a government of the people. It's a government of the overwhelmingly rich, of the corporations and the wealthy.... And so it does what they want." He explained that big business is interested in short-term gain and cares little about what are called, in the economics literature, *externalities* (consequences that are not part of market transactions). In other words large corporations are self-interested and unconcerned with making a deal that's good for everyone. For example, a company that manufactures or sells cars is not worried about pollution, traffic congestion, accidents and injuries, said Chomsky.

He noted the financial crisis of 2008 is a prime example of people ignoring externalities. "This [economic collapse] is what happened when Goldman Sachs, JP Morgan Chase, Barclays Bank and the rest of them made fraudulent or semi-fraudulent [transactions] in the housing market to try to maximize short term gain."

An effect of this is what's called *systemic risk*, meaning the danger that one company getting into trouble can spread and destroy the whole system. In the financial world, systemic risk is not lethal because the public can bail a company out. "So AIG didn't go bust as it should have, and Goldman Sachs didn't collapse as it should have," Chomsky observed. In the case of Earth's natural environment, however, the risk of destruction is high but an executive with Exxon Mobil or an official at the Chamber of Commerce is focused on short-term gains so externalities are ignored. "And there's nobody to bail you out."

"Market systems are designed to create lethal catastrophes," Chomsky warned. These market systems and structures can be overcome with regulation, government control and popular pressure, in theory, but all of these require a political democracy, and one of the effects of a high concentration of capital inequality is that democracy is weakened.

Chomsky pointed out that the American public favors higher expenditures and efforts to deal with climate change, but that doesn't matter. "What matters is what the rich and powerful think." And they are quite transparent in their opposition to such expenditures. "The American Chamber of Commerce, the business lobby, the petroleum lobbies have openly proclaimed they are carrying out efforts to undermine popular beliefs in anthropogenic climate change." He referred to the organization called ALEC—American Legislative Exchange Council—that creates legislative programs for states in the US[6] and recently rolled out a school program they call *balanced teaching*. The name may sound nice, but it means in practice that if a Grade 6 class is given "information" about climate change, that information has to be balanced by "information" about climate denial, which comes out of Exxon Mobil. "It's like a totalitarian state," said Chomsky, "It's a way of ensuring that the public is as stupid and

> **If you can't answer an argument, shriek.**
> **That's true in corporate relations, true in**
> **international relations. Just rant. Call people names.**
> **Slander them. Anything to undermine**
> **an argument you can't respond to.**
>
> **NOAM CHOMSKY**

ignorant as possible, and it makes perfect sense from the business lobby point of view."

I described the Canadian oil industry's appeal to Americans to buy Canadian oil because it's more ethical. I explained how this campaign surprised me because it is the message we are used to hearing from the American Petroleum Institute or the US Chamber of Commerce, not something we normally hear in Canada. Chomsky responded that in recent years Canada has abandoned many of its more decent characteristics. "Canada used to be a relatively tolerant, open society and less violent than the US. There's plenty of crime, but was much more moderate and humane than in the South.... But that's changed in recent years."

He believes this change happened, in part, because of the North America Free Trade Agreement, which has brought Canadian and American societies closer at an economic level and increased the power of the corporate sector in both countries at the expense of the general population. "It's also due to policies which are quite openly driving Canada to the right. Canada has changed in international affairs and many other things."

When it comes to rancorous debate, Chomsky sees the same pollution of the public square on both sides of the border. "If you can't answer an argument, shriek. That's true in corporate relations, true in international relations. Just rant. Call people names. Slander them. Anything to undermine an argument you can't respond to." He said there are no magic keys, no simple ways out of such issues, whether it's slavery, women's rights or the environment. "It's going to be a long, hard struggle."

Despite the structural failings of corporations, Joel Bakan believes change is possible, but the solution ultimately has to come from us: "We need to feel we have the right and the obligation as citizens in the public domain of democracy to do something about this." This is critically important, and why I am writing this book. People need to become savvier about the systems we're creating, more aware of how propaganda works and how public discourse gets polluted.

It occurred to me how wrong-headed the demonization of corporate leaders is. We invented corporations for good reasons—to raise immense amounts of capital to build infrastructure such as bridges, railways and air transportation systems. But we also made them furiously focused on creating shareholder value, and in the wake of the anti-regulation movement that started with Thatcher and Reagan we removed many balancing mechanisms and constraining regulations. Corporate CEOs are required to make money for their shareholders, and if they fail to do so they can be in serious trouble, even legally.

No doubt there are some greedy psychopaths at the helm of a few large companies, but there is a much deeper, systemic problem here. Increasing deregulation and unchecked corporate independence, combined with legal constructs that encourage the pathological nature of these institutions, means they can and must act in the interest of shareholders, sometimes to the detriment of communities and the environment. When things go wrong with products—when it's found that tobacco causes cancer, or oil and gas are changing the climate, when their license to operate is threatened—they are of course motivated to become skilled at propaganda.

The result is a more corrupted debate, more misleading PR and advertising being pumped into the public square. It can be relentless, not because corporate leaders are bad guys but because it's systemic, and large companies have deep pockets. By allowing corporations to self-regulate we place them in a position where they may actually have a corporate responsibility to their shareholders to pollute the public sphere. Corporations are motivated to manipulate public opinion and perception because when things go wrong, if they don't, shareholders may be outraged by poor stock prices or the companies might lose their licenses to operate. Massive amounts of advertising dollars are being spent by big business on the organized manipulation of public opinion, and in the next chapter we will see what happens when governments get involved—and help them.

9

A Case Study:
Foreign-Funded Radicals

THE WORLD'S LARGEST reservoir of crude bitumen—a thick, sticky hydrocarbon with the viscosity of cold molasses that smells and looks like tar—is located in northern Alberta, Canada, in a vast area larger than England. Formed over millions of years, small amounts of this gummy substance were used centuries ago by Cree Aboriginals to waterproof their canoes, but in 1967 a massive commercial operation began to release the energy that was locked into these deposits. Separating the heavy petroleum product from sand has been a challenge, but more difficult still has been the contentious dispute surrounding this valuable resource and how it will be transported to markets.

This controversy is alarming because it stalls action, and the threat of global warming is no longer just seen in ice core samples or minute laboratory measurements. It is larger than life, right before our eyes. In 2015, the world's seven billion inhabitants went through the hottest year ever recorded;[1] drought gripped California, where the snowpack vital for water supplies fell to its lowest level in five centuries;[2] more than 4,000 people died in heat waves in India[3] and Pakistan[4] as temperatures hit 120°F (49°C); Cyclone Chapala battered Yemen[5]—a country that has never seen a cyclone hit its shores—drenching some areas with seven year's worth of rain in

48 hours. That same year, the far eastern Pacific spawned Hurricane Patricia, thought to be the strongest storm ever recorded;[6] and rising ocean temperatures caused the third mass coral bleaching event in recorded history (following ones in 1998 and 2010), killing an estimated 4,600 square miles of coral around the globe.[7] Never has there been a greater disparity between what scientists say we should be concerned about and what members of government and the oil and gas industry are doing.

In this case study I highlight several extreme examples of polarizing spin and misleading propaganda that epitomize the extent to which the vested interests that Joel Bakan and Noam Chomsky described—and governments that support them—will go to confuse issues and discredit critics, on both sides of the Canada-US border.

A few years ago, Canadians attuned to such things noticed a peculiar shift in the international debate about the environmental impact and economic importance of this country's best-known natural resource. Phrases such as "ethical oil" bubbled to the surface as oil industry proponents sought to defend not only the resource, but also the proposed Keystone and Enbridge Northern Gateway pipelines that would carry crude to the Gulf of Mexico or British Columbia's northern coast for export to Asia. At the same time, First Nations and environmental groups that dared speak out against either the oil sands or the pipelines proposed to carry its crude were labeled by the Harper government and the oil and gas industry as "foreign-funded radicals," bent on undermining Canada's sovereignty and economic growth.

And then the peculiar term "ethical oil" started being used on national television. One day while watching a CBC interview, I remember EthicalOil.org spokesperson Kathryn Marshall repeating it like a mantra. She had a slightly unhinged tone, like a comedian on *Saturday Night Live*, as she refused again and again to answer the interviewer's questions about who was funding EthicalOil.org. Marshall tried to deflect the question with pat statements about puppet groups trying to hijack a Canadian pipeline process. Her desperate and comical efforts became a YouTube sensation, and her urgent plea to stop the so-called foreign-funded radicals ran on media outlets from coast to coast for weeks.[8]

In one interview, Marshall said Northern Gateway is good for Canada and will allow the export of, "more of our ethically produced oil to different countries that can reduce their dependency on conflict oil from nations like Nigeria and Saudi Arabia and Iran that have atrocious human rights records and really don't care about the environment at all." She said ethical oil supporters should, "make sure that foreign interests and their foreign-funded front groups and lobby groups" didn't interfere with the pipeline approval and didn't "hijack a Canadian process."[9]

As the ethical oil, foreign-funded radicals propaganda campaign rolled out, I listened closely to the rhetoric and shook my head as I watched the media's lapdog response. In spite of a lack of evidence of any wrongdoing on the part of environmental or community groups, the media seemed to play along with everything that was said. It was an astonishing—and apparently very successful—overreach.

Conservative Canadian Senator Nicole Eaton charged so-called foreign-funded radicals with political manipulation: "There is influence peddling. There are millions of dollars crossing the borders masquerading as charitable donations." She then launched a senate inquiry into the funding of environmental charities by foreign foundations, alleging they were, "audaciously treading on our domestic affairs and on Canadian sovereignty."[10] The Canadian Press started digging and revealed that most Canadian charities receive foreign funds, including many well outside the environmental realm. The CP analysis found that only one of the top ten foreign-funded charities could be considered a conservation group—Ducks Unlimited Canada—while CARE Canada, which fights poverty in developing countries, reported the most foreign funding at about $99 million.[11] Amid these attacks by Conservative critics, it was revealed that the Canada Revenue Agency was auditing environmental groups that the Harper government had marked as enemies.[12]

There was even a suggestion of money laundering from Environment Minister Peter Kent, while Senator Don Plett asked about
environmentalists: "...Where would they draw the line on where
they receive money from? Will they take money from Al Qaeda,
the Hamas or the Taliban? Who is really making the decisions in
Canada if we allow foreign money to lobby against what should be
Canadian made decisions?"[13]

Adversarial debate is an important democratic tool, but combative discourse is a problem when it is used to demonize, to obscure
truth and steamroll dissent. As Steve Rosell, Roger Conner, Bruno
Latour and Noam Chomsky have all pointed out, when campaigns
do this the result is public confusion, polarization and gridlock. And
let's be clear, similar campaigns take place globally around all kinds
of big issues—everything from gun control, tobacco and hydraulic
fracturing to weapons of mass destruction—led by political parties
and corporations.

Over the following months I watched as the PR pollution grew
more toxic and the echo chamber resonated. Attacks against scientists escalated and a 2013 survey found 90 percent of federal government scientists in Canada felt they could not speak freely to the
media, while 86 percent believed they would face censure or retalia-
tion if they did. The survey of more than 4,000 scientists, commis-
sioned by the Professional Institute of the Public Service of Canada,
published in a report called *The Big Chill*, found almost one in four
said they had been asked to exclude or alter technical information.[14]

I have taken on my share of PR battles over the years as head of
my own public relations company, Hoggan & Associates. In fact, my
Vancouver-based firm has a reputation for working on tough issues
and sometimes taking opponents to the mat. When it comes to reputation management we are known for hard-nosed tactics, and we
have faced off with governments, unions and environmental groups.
But even to me, these strategies used to defend tar sands oil and oil
pipelines seemed excessive.

What Harper's government and the oil industry were promoting showed a serious disconnect with Canadian values, since almost 80 percent of Canadians I surveyed wanted stricter laws to protect the environment.[15] This PR campaign seemed to have been borrowed straight from the Harper government's allies at the Ethical Oil Institute, founded by controversial former tobacco lobbyist Ezra Levant, who himself borrowed from the US Republican Tea Party playbook. Levant devised a plan to brand Alberta's oil sands as "fair trade," versus the "conflict oil" of regimes supporting terrorism. He claimed, "Ethical oil is like fair trade coffee or conflict-free diamonds. Ethical oil burns the same as conflict oil in your gas tank and it costs the same, but it's morally superior and some people value that."[16]

In a book on the topic, Levant wrote: "If our goal as moral citizens is to make the world a better place, then there is only one choice: to pump as much oil as we possibly can out of Fort McMurray. Pump and steam and dig and drill and get that oil out of the sand in any and every way we can." He further noted, "Every drop of oil from Alberta is one less drop from some fascist theocracy, or some brutal warlord; one less cent into the treasuries of Russia's secret police and al-Qaeda's murderers."[17]

Environmentalists poured plenty of gasoline on this controversy too. The Sierra Club compared the tar sands to heroin, and protesters at various events carried placards that read, "Tar Sands Kill" and "Tar Sands Oil is Blood Oil."[18] A 2012 campaign attacked fossil fuel companies with the slogan, "Exxon hates your children."[19] None of this rhetoric was helpful.

Levant wrote about protestors in his blog: "If we were to take their advice (environmentalists) and shut down the oil sands, we'd simply be handing billions of dollars of business to misogynistic, terrorist-financing, nuclear bomb-building, union-busting, gay-bashing dictatorships like Saudi Arabia, Iran, etc."[20]

Meanwhile, the world was continuing to warm, and the Conference Board of Canada ranked Canada 15th overall in environmental stewardship among the 17 richest nations in the world.[21] Our failure to reduce greenhouse gas emissions placed us dead last among G-8 countries;[22] Canada's Arctic exceeded worst-case scenarios, with the most extreme sea ice melt in recorded history.[23]

In 2012 the Harper government passed Omnibus Budget Bill C-38, which was called the *Jobs, Growth and Long-Term Prosperity Act*. This sweeping bill was widely seen as an attack on environmental protection and science. The bill changed 70 federal laws and, concealing major amendments in a budget, made discussion of any single provision difficult. Protection of fish habitat and species at risk were reduced in Canada's *Fisheries Act*. Thousands of bodies of water, lakes and streams across the country were removed from oversight as Canada's *Navigable Waters Protection Act* became a *Navigation Protection Act*. The former *Canadian Environmental Assessment Act* was repealed and a new act proclaimed that enabled fast-track approval of pipelines and oil sands expansion. In the same massive piece of legislation, the country's only high Arctic data collection facility, the Polar Environmental Atmospheric Research Laboratory, was closed, and the government removed Canada from the international Kyoto Protocol agreement.[24]

Canada now protects less than 1 percent of its oceans compared with Australia, for instance, which has a comprehensive network of marine protected areas covering 40 percent of its oceans.[25]

Few PR campaigns in Canada have been as extreme or well funded as the one I have outlined here, and I've certainly never seen one as cocky. But it would be a mistake to dismiss it as a crazy sideshow or to think this only happens in Canada. In fact, this kind of oil and gas industry propaganda seems to have been born in the United States.

US Examples

The US firm Edelman—one of the largest PR firms in the world— was hired by TransCanada Corporation in 2014 after that company was stalled in its attempt to build the Keystone XL pipeline from Alberta to the US Gulf Coast. The PR giant was tasked with promoting an alternative route to carry crude oil from the Alberta tar sands to east coast refineries—entirely within Canada. The proposed pipeline would carry 1.1 million barrels per day of western Canadian crude to eastern refineries and export facilities, through some existing converted pipelines in Ontario as well as new pipeline through Quebec and New Brunswick.

Details of this aggressive PR campaign were revealed when Greenpeace Canada managed to obtain copies of draft documents that showed Edelman's strategy to garner public support for the $12-billion Energy East project. It included creating so-called grassroots advocacy groups to discredit and distract environmental groups that might jeopardize the proposed 2,858-mile project.[26]

Greenpeace's Keith Stewart characterized the firm's tactics as "dirty tricks" and said the documents exposed how worried the company was about the Energy East pipeline facing as much flak as the Keystone or Northern Gateway projects.[27] Edelman's strategy would counter opponents by "distracting them from their mission and causing them to redirect their resources," and by working with "supportive third parties who can in turn put the pressure on, particularly when TransCanada can't." The strategy would target groups such as the Council of Canadians, Ecology Ottawa and the David Suzuki Foundation (as well as their funders) and investigate any litigation issues or audits they might be facing. Edelman suggested this could be accomplished through *opposition research*, a term used to describe digging up dirt on your opponents.[28] It's a common tactic in US politics, but I wondered why it was being used as a weapon against ordinary citizens.

Edelman is used to controversy. The firm was at the center of a firestorm of trouble in 2006 after its founder, Richard Edelman, apologized for his firm using fake grassroots bloggers in a union fight with Wal-Mart.[29] The company also ran a $52-million campaign for the American Petroleum Institute that allegedly involved pro-industry citizens' groups. The "Energy Citizens" campaign was designed to appear as if generated by ordinary people, but it was actually masterminded and run by oil company lobbyists.[30]

In the document entitled *Strategic Plan: Quebec*, the PR giant drafted plans to recruit "third-party" voices to help build an echo chamber of "aligned voices" and while the company's founder denied working with astroturf groups, Kert Davies, executive director of the Climate Investigations Center, was quoted in a *Huffington Post* article in late 2014 as saying this was precisely what was happening. "If astroturf is using artificial grassroots to support a corporate agenda, this is clearly it." He added it's not often you see "the full battle plan" of a major industry PR effort, but said this was a small window into the workings of big oil company campaigns.[31]

Astroturfing involves creating fake grassroots groups and makes it almost impossible to distinguish between a legitimate groundswell and manufactured opinion. Some PR companies use such groups to garner synthetic support, to alter public perception or simply stir up doubt. On the Internet astroturfing sometimes takes the form of bogus endorsements for products, hotels or restaurants, but in the larger sphere blogs and comments appear as seemingly spontaneous expressions of support, but are in fact, masterminded and funded by big business, oil companies, chemical companies and more. In his book *Grassroots for Hire*, author Edward Walker defines this kind of false public participation as an elite campaign masquerading as a mass movement.[32]

"Win nasty or lose pretty...Screw your enemy...Push fear and anger," and above all always work to give corporate cash "total anonymity:" these are playbook mantras of another of big business's hired PR guns in the United States. Richard Berman is a Washington-based lawyer and political consultant whose stock in trade is exploiting fear and anger in what he has called "an endless war" against environmentalists. His PR game plan was exposed in 2014 when a speech to oil and gas industry officials was secretly recorded. *The New York Times* broke the story after Berman spoke to the Western Energy Alliance in Colorado Springs.[33]

Among other zingers in the leaked audio, Berman said, "If the oil and gas industry wants to prevent its opponents from slowing its efforts to drill in more places, it must be prepared to employ tactics like digging up embarrassing tidbits about environmentalists and liberal celebrities." His public affairs firm, Berman & Company, prides itself on exploiting fear, greed and anger, and in the secretly taped speech he urged executives not to worry about offending people: "You can win ugly or lose pretty." The master of astroturfing explained he receives "anonymous" donations from businesses and has used the funds to create dozens of nonprofit groups that appear arm's length from industry, independent and community based. These front groups launch spin campaigns to influence public opinion against environmental advocates or industry critics.

"We run this stuff through nonprofit organizations that are insulated from having to disclose donors," he told the Colorado Springs meeting. "There is total anonymity. People don't know who supports us." During the meeting he also advised the group that for $3 million he could battle their environmental foes with his Big Green Radicals campaign. This is just one in his network of front groups and so-called think tanks that he launched to block food safety legislation, to undermine environmental advocacy groups such as the Sierra Club or groups opposed to fracking. Other pointers he offered the audience included using humor to marginalize opponents and tearing down celebrities by playing up their hypocrisy.

Misleading, deceptive PR campaigns have been used for decades in the US. The Americans had clean coal long before Canadians had ethical oil.

The term *clean coal* was coined in the late 1980s to deflect public concern from a dirty form of energy. The words were echoed by front groups with names such as Citizens for a Sound Economy, the Clean and Safe Energy Coalition and the Advancement of Sound Science Coalition. The Western Fuels Association teamed with the National Coal Association in 1991 to form the Information Council on the Environment, aiming to "reposition global warming as a theory (not a fact)" and "supply alternative facts to support that global warming would be good."[34]

Let's be clear, there is no such thing as clean coal. The green-washing term sells the idea that coal is somehow environmentally friendly. The burning of coal combined with mist from the Thames Valley is what gave London, England its infamous pea soupers, the black fogs that were a lethal combination of soot particles and sulfur dioxide. London's Great Smog of 1952 killed an estimated 12,000 people in five days, and left another 100,000 in respiratory distress. It also led to reductions in coal burning in England.[35] Coal pollution continues to take a deadly toll, and according to the American Lung Association, 13,000 people die prematurely every year because of it.[36] Coal-fired power plants in the US burn more than a billion tons annually, emitting more CO_2 per unit of energy than any other fuel. The industry contaminates drinking water, is a leading cause of acid rain and is the largest source of mercury pollution in the US.[37]

Clean coal is a myth perpetrated by industry PR and bankrolled by mining companies such as Peabody Energy, Duke Energy and the Union Pacific Railroad. An advertising agency called R&R Partners is credited with coming up with the clean coal oxymoron—and is also responsible for the slogan "what happens in Las Vegas, stays in Las Vegas."[38]

Another PR company, the Virginia-based Hawthorn Group, worked on behalf of the American Coalition for Clean Coal Electricity to spread the gospel of clean coal, and subcontracted the Washington firm of Bonner & Associates to help fight the Waxman-Markey Bill, which proposed limits on total greenhouse gases. The bill was approved by the House of Representatives in 2009 but defeated, in part, because of the astroturfing efforts of Bonner. The PR company was later accused of defrauding the federal government, and in 2009 Bonner acknowledged that his firm had forged more than a dozen anti-climate bill letters that were sent to members of the US Congress. The fraudulent letters, on fake letterhead, were intended to look as if they had come from minority groups opposed to the Waxman-Markey Bill.[39]

Trying to brand oil as ethical or coal as clean seems blatantly absurd, yet millions are spent on these campaigns because they sometimes work, not to persuade but to obscure and polarize (but more on that in following chapters). This is not just PR, it is propaganda, and I offer these examples here because they illustrate how far some corporations and institutions will go to block legislation, to push pipelines and to muzzle scientists.

By attacking the credibility of scientists and creating doubt about their findings—without actually doing any science themselves—critics poison the well of democracy and flood the public square with misinformation. These kinds of campaigns use abusive ad hominem attacks on the character of opponents in order to invalidate the concerns of scientists and environmental groups. If the media or public is duped into talking about foreign-funded radicals, then the discussion is no longer about climate change, tanker traffic or pipelines. Through repetition these assaults feed biases, stereotypes and prejudices, stirring up powerful feelings and distorted thinking. They are part of a public communication problem we should all be aware of and expect our leaders to shrink from.

As the interviews and conversations for this book continued, it became more and more clear this was a serious problem, and while these examples revolve around climate change—as that's an area I'm familiar with—such toxic forces are at work in many areas. Frankly, these tactics leave me speechless, because I know the vast resources and amount of work that goes into organizing them, and getting away with it. They should leave us all speechless, but we need to move beyond being speechless and take a closer at what's happening. We can't be truly effective in the public square without understanding these destructive and pathological barriers to honest communication and debate. In the following chapters we will learn more about the process of propaganda, about silencing techniques, about gaslighting and other assaults on democracy, to gain a better understanding of this serious form of pollution and ways to deal with it.

10

Assault On Democracy

with ALEX HIMELFARB

To better understand the significance of extraordinary campaigns like those described in the case study, we must now look at the role politics plays in today's over-heated climate of acrimonious debate. When public discourse is invaded by this kind of warlike political PR and the kind of personal attacks generally reserved for elections, the opportunity for authentic debate evaporates. And if we blame the situation on a lack of facts, a failure to communicate, or partisan polarization we're not looking at the whole picture.

I had invited Alex Himelfarb, a renowned social scientist and one of Canada's leading political pundits, to speak at a David Suzuki Foundation board dinner, and while strolling back to our hotel we discussed the foreign-funded radicals campaign as well as the over-the-top PR generated by the oil and gas industry and Canada's Conservative government. I remarked upon how odd it was that then Prime Minister Harper, who was said to be highly intelligent, could be ignoring climate change, dragging his feet on regulating greenhouse gas emissions from the oil sands and taking such a combative approach to community groups opposed to pipelines and tankers. I suggested that Harper was either not as smart as people say he is, or just evil.

Himelfarb responded, "Why the urge to demonize or diminish? Why would we want to buy in, however tempting, to the prevalent and corrosive junk politics that sees a world of heroes, villains and fools?"[1]

That stopped me, and got me thinking about how risky it is to view people behind such campaigns as dense or immoral. I understood Himelfarb was saying the situation required an entirely different attitude—and again I stress that such an insight isn't helpful only on the Canadian side of the border. The problem of pollution in the public square is not a simple linear equation that can be quickly solved. It involves a complex set of variables and elements—and governance, or the lack of it, is a key factor.

The potential for positive dialogue hinges on our ability to bring collective issues to the table, said Himelfarb, who had a long career as a federal public servant, was secretary to the cabinet and clerk of the privy council serving three prime ministers.

Himelfarb believes that the Right prefers to shut down public discourse and that modern life makes it easy for this to happen. We live increasingly privatized lives, with scant time to devote to public policy. Issues of the common good often don't make it to the table. "Time is short. Mostly we're just trying to get by, deal with the kids who have a cold, pay our mortgage." It is increasingly difficult to engage people on issues like inequality, poverty or climate change. "From our private milieu they seem pretty abstract; they don't seem immediate." Another reason collective issues don't make it to the table is that we spend less and less of our lives in public spaces interacting with people who have different views and experiences so that we can develop a sense of the common good. Divisive politics and growing inequality conspire to undermine social trust. These elements play perfectly into the right wing's hand.

Himelfarb explained that there is no evidence that Canadians have in fact moved to the Right. There are perhaps 20 percent who would self-identify as being on the Right and a similar number who would identify as being on the Left. But most have no wings, either

**Minimize public spaces where
dialogue might occur and where it does occur,
confuse it, obscure it.
The idea is to kill the debate, not foster it.**

ALEX HIMELFARB

right or left, and instead have internally competing Right and Left values.

In Canada, the federal Conservatives didn't need to convince the public of anything or win any debate; they just needed to avoid the debate. He called this do-nothing stance the default position, or *gravity*. In an age of heightened individualism and consumerism, it's pretty easy to undermine trust in public institutions. In an age of uncertainty, it's pretty easy to undermine trust in those who are different or to feed fear. To have a serious, moral debate and do something about fear and distrust requires an *anti-gravity* position, which is so-called because it takes energy, hard work and a real sense of the common good. Himelfarb explained that going along with gravity is easy. A number of thinkers have made the case that, without a crisis, we prefer to go with the flow, and that is the major reason we don't get action on the environment. We have a bias toward what is, the status quo. Making change is hard work.

The easiest thing for the Right to do is to spoil the public space and inhibit debate, to limit the public's capacity and will, Himelfarb explained. They don't have to convince the public that climate change isn't real. They just have to make it seem that all the proponents are pursuing their special interests—just as we all do—sowing doubt that anybody is telling the whole truth and then exaggerating the hazards of solutions to make them seem unbelievably risky. "The Right doesn't need to win hearts and minds, it just needs to make sure the Left doesn't. The key is to sow doubt and limit our sense of what's possible."

Like many others I interviewed, Alex Himelfarb noted the increasing and effective use of a classic rhetorical ploy called *ad hominem*—where attacks are aimed at a person's character, not their line of reasoning. This tactic can muzzle the voices of scientists and close down neutral bodies and scientific initiatives that might result in believable data or even parliamentary debate. All proponents have to do is close down public debate.

What we are seeing is an attack on democracy, and Himelfarb stressed that playing the same game isn't the answer. Progressives won't score any goals unless they have a better counter approach. Himelfarb suggested several strategic moves.

First, paint a picture of a better future. The Right has been very effective at undermining everything that looks like a positive vision of the future, or at least the possibility that we could ever hope to achieve anything close to positive. Most citizens want a greener and more just Canada.[2] The questions then become, Do we think that such a Canada is likely or even possible? Do we trust one another and our institutions to believe we will all play our part? Environmentalists who hope to inspire people by prophecies of doom are actually feeding into a sense of fear. Himelfarb suggests that we create a compelling narrative and express why the public ought to care. Environmentalists must explain why every previous generation did what was necessary to secure the infrastructure and climate for people to succeed, and emphasize this generation's obligation to do the same. Learn to get better at the art of persuasion, and don't be put into the conservative position that protecting what we have is the best that we can do, explained Himelfarb. Also avoid polarization and present more voices across the spectrum, for example, by bringing environmentalists, social and labor advocates together.

The Right has been very effective in promoting a vision of the world as nothing more than an arena for competitive individualism in which ordinary people are consumers and taxpayers rather than citizens with mutual and shared responsibility. Himelfarb pointed to British Prime Minister Margaret Thatcher's infamous "there is no such thing as society" comment, which framed all problems in terms of individual blame and merit, in which the rich deserve their wealth and the poor their poverty, in which there are no systemic problems or collective solutions.[3] Himelfarb argued that at the very time when our collective problems are most challenging, our collective toolkit is inadequate.

Himelfarb reminded me that a few decades ago, the sociologist C. Wright Mills described sociological imagination as the ability to link private troubles and public issues.[4] That pretty well captures the progressive challenge: reconnecting people to collective solutions. Alex Himelfarb urged progressives to become hugely better at telling a positive narrative that expands what people see as possible, that engages people and gives them a plausible, feasible alternative to the status quo. And, he argued, we have to rebuild the public space where it's possible to hear a moral discourse and moral narratives that link to people's everyday lives, for example, to their roles as parents.

Further, progressives must call the Right out on PR spin and its assault on democratic institutions. Democracy depends on engaged and informed citizenship. Any attack on reason, on information and on debate is an attack on democracy. And the notion that there is no society or "this is not a time to commit sociology" (as former Canadian Prime Minister Stephen Harper said in 2013)[5] undermines engagement on public issues. "We believe that if people had the information, knowledge and the ability to participate in these debates, they would not accept what's going on and that's what the Right is worried about. For progressives, the key is restoring confidence that progress built on the best available evidence is not just desirable but possible. Of course we need to reengage on the moral debates."

But, said Himelfarb, most importantly we have to reject the line that there is no alternative to the current market triumphalism and austerity. Indeed, whenever politicians tell us there is no alternative, we can be assured there is, and it's likely one we would prefer, were it on offer. To turn things around is to expand our sense of what's possible. "And, notwithstanding the growing evidence that facts don't change people's minds, that emotion is the key to change, our best bet to turn things around is still an informed and engaged democracy—and that means opposing, at every turn, the attack on reason, on experts and expertise, on evidence and science."

And finally, he proposed, we need to realize that we are in a long game, not a short game. One speech or one clever strategy cannot turn the world around. We need to keep acting over and over again—not just focusing on the next election. Incessant repetition is something the Right has been doing very well, Alex Himelfarb concluded.

11

Silencing the Voices of Others

with JASON STANLEY

JASON STANLEY is a professor of philosophy and epistemology with a PhD from MIT. He teaches courses on democracy and propaganda at Yale. He is also an academic who explores new ideas and techniques about mass deception that are directly related to pollution in the public square.

Stanley explained there are a number of rhetorical and linguistic tactics that are being used now to silence people, and one of the most blatant is the misappropriation of words such as *ethical* or *clean* in relation to oil or coal. In an article he wrote in the *New York Times'* Stone series, Stanley said that using what he called code words to win support has always been part of the arsenal of politics, but it is now widely used in the popular media.[1]

When we met to talk, Stanley explained that making outlandish allegations, twisting meanings and making improbable statements has the same effect. This is not really about making substantive claims; it's what he calls a linguistic strategy for stealing the voices of others, silencing people. Making bizarre claims that President Obama is a secret Islamist agent, or was born in Kenya, painted the US President as grossly insincere. His voice was stolen, not by a legitimate objection to his platform or an argument, but by undermining the public's trust in him so that nothing he said could be taken at face value. Simply put, when Fox News carried a story charging that Obama is really a secret Muslim[2] it damaged everyone's sincerity, and any opportunity for reasoned debate evaporated. Similar propaganda techniques were at work when First Nations and environmentalists in Canada were called foreign-funded radicals.

It's a simple tactic: When the public doesn't trust you and you can't rely on your own credibility to argue your views, when the public doesn't share your values or interests, when facts aren't on your side, why not attack and undermine your opponents' integrity while making them appear to have a vested interest?

When no audience or viewer expects truth in the media, only bias, political candidates cannot be held responsible for lying. Stanley made the case that it then becomes possible to lie in public with impunity; there is no downside to deceit. Every person has an "everyone's doing it" defense. People start to believe that no one is speaking authentically—that even scientists are massaging data to suit their ideological agendas.

Jason Stanley calls such strategy an attack on objective speech. When scientists' facts are twisted, when everyone is trying to either complicate issues unnecessarily or promote a political agenda, public dialogue becomes confused. The people can be led to believe that "Climate scientists are just trying to get us to wear healthy clothing, or eat vegetarian food.... They are trying to change American cultural norms. They are just trying to sway you, not inform you about what is going on."[3]

In the PR business, I have found there can be pressure to oversimplify issues, and the clarity of philosophical analysis is helpful—which is why I appreciated the precision of Jason Stanley's fresh way of thinking.

Stanley dives deeply into issues that Alex Himelfarb raised and believes that the right wing media, such as Fox News, is not trying to communicate accurate, well-researched stories, but is scrambling information, broadcasting noise so that it becomes difficult to hear the truth. This insight came to him a few years ago, when he was watching Fox News and began thinking about its claim of being "fair and balanced," something he and his friends thought nobody believed, including Fox News. He decided that much of the right wing news media is not trying to deliver fair and balanced coverage of events or reportage of issues. Instead, the message of Rupert Murdoch's media corporations goes something like this: In a world where everyone is trying to manipulate everyone else for their own interests and where no one can believe anything they hear, there is no point in being fair, no possibility of balance. Nobody is trustworthy.

Stanley argued further that Fox engages in a kind of silencing tactic when describing itself as "fair and balanced," especially to an audience that is perfectly aware that it is neither. The effect is to suggest there is no possibility of balanced news, only propaganda; this results in a silencing of all news sources by suggesting everyone is grossly insincere.

Stanley warned that democracy is in danger when we no longer expect truth or demand accountability from public figures, when for many there is no longer even a pretense of integrity. One early warning sign is when an institution "has a problem" with facts; facts don't align with its interests, and a critic may have more credibility. The climate change debate is rife with examples of this, Stanley told me.

Public discourse has deteriorated to such an extent that the traditional debating model—based on accuracy, evidence and proof—isn't happening, so the typical fallback position is to tarnish another person's reputation. When it comes to climate change, for instance, the new technique is to first criticize the research and scholarship, then undermine and discredit scientists. How is this done? Rather than engaging in reasoned discourse and challenging facts, Stanley believes the general strategy is to co-opt vocabulary.

"It is difficult to have a reasoned debate about the costs and benefits of a policy when one side has seized control of the linguistic means to express all positive claims." This kind of dexterous management of language was brilliantly highlighted in the writings of George Orwell, whose Newspeak was designed by a one-party state to prevent freethinking.[4] Stanley said the diaries of Polish-born journalist and comparative literature professor Victor Klemperer are another rich resource when detailing this kind of propaganda.[5] Drawing on his experience in Germany from 1933 to 1945, the linguist recorded how propaganda changed the value of words. For instance "special treatment" became a euphemism for murder; "intensified interrogation" another name for torture, and words such as "fanatical" were elevated to the rank of high praise.

It is difficult to have a sensible debate about a policy's benefits versus costs when the policy is labeled "Operation Iraqi Freedom" or "tax relief." Co-opted language takes many forms, even as oxymorons such as "clean coal" or "ethical oil." Stanley explained that seizing control of positive vocabulary makes naysayers appear to oppose something that is clearly beneficial. "It's possible to silence people by denying them access to the vocabulary to express their claims."

Democracy works only if reasoned debate in the public square is possible. If everything is mislabeled, then conditions for deliberative democracy do not exist. If people are deluded into thinking there is such a thing as clean coal, or ethical oil, if their ability to apply correct facts is circumvented, and the credibility of experts is undercut, where is the basis for reasoned debate? It's like trying to design a building without a level.

Stanley became concerned about the role of silencing in the public sphere through analyzing right wing media and its reliance on *truthiness*—a word coined by satirist Stephen Colbert to describe the "feeling" of truth based on a gut reaction, rather than evidence or logic.[6] Stanley explained that when citizens have no access to reliable news they become suspicious and untrusting: "The effects of a belief in general gross insincerity are apparent in societies in which the state media delivers only propaganda. Citizens who grow up in a state where authorities deliver propaganda have no experience with trust." In such an authoritarian society, "The public's trust in public speech, whether by politicians or in the media, disintegrates to such

**Democracy works only
if you have normal, reasoned debate...
so you need to set the conditions
where that's possible.**

JASON STANLEY

a degree that it undermines the possibility of straightforward communication in the public sphere."

Stanley used the example of North Korea: "Clearly something is really wrong with discussion in the public sphere in North Korea." No one trusts anyone and no one believes what anyone says because they assume it is propaganda. We would hope that free speech guarantees the conditions for deliberative democracy. But if that is true, "How did we end up with public spaces in North America where nobody trusts what anyone says, and that look in certain aspects like North Korea—even though we've got free speech? That's a real mystery."

The answer is, when everyone has the right to make up his or her own facts it weakens everyone's ability to speak with integrity, and he concludes: Free speech alone is not sufficient for delivering the conditions for reasoned debate. It is impossible without trust and sincerity, and Stanley suggests this is the first critical piece in the puzzle he calls *The Ways of Silencing*.

The whole "ethical oil" campaign in Canada sprang up after many, many years during which climate change was largely ignored by the oil and gas industry and Canada's Conservative government. Then suddenly, legislation started to pop up in Europe and California, and influential companies like Wal-Mart started looking at low-carbon produce. The European Union threatened to stigmatize Canadian oil by proposing a Fuel Quality Directive designed to curb greenhouse gas emissions, and at one point sought to label all oil from the tar sands as particularly dirty, which would have made European re-finers less likely to import it. When California passed a Low Carbon Fuel Standard, the Alberta oil industry and related US groups began pushing for bills to limit other states from passing similar standards.

Suddenly the Canadian government and oil producers couldn't ignore the trending legislation any longer. They needed an offensive position, and so they came up with the allegation that foreign-funded radicals were attacking Canada's "ethical oil." Suddenly at home, criticism of Canadian oil producers could be interpreted as a threat to Canadian prosperity and sovereignty, and the new frame had the added advantage of putting the environmental community on the defensive.

This kind of frame can effectively silence opposition because it prevents people from communicating their message. Debates were no longer about tankers or climate change. Opponents had to re-fute claims that they were money laundering; NGOs had to spend enormous amounts of time explaining themselves. This messag-ing was not aimed at revealing the truth. It was aimed at silencing critics and diverting the public discourse. Suddenly the Northern Gateway Pipeline wasn't about Enbridge's safety track record or potential spills affecting shellfish—it was about foreign funding and sovereignty.

12

Gaslighting Blurs Our Reality

with BRYANT WELCH

SOLUTIONS TO THE current environmental communication problems outlined in my earlier Case Study include figuring out forms of communication that are eloquent and persuasive and help people understand more—not less. We don't need people playing mind games, Harvard-trained lawyer, psychologist, lobbyist and author Bryant Welch explained to me. Welch wrote about a technique he calls *gaslighting* in his book *State of Confusion*.[1]

The term gaslighting comes from a classic 1944 thriller called *Gaslight*, in which a manipulative husband tries to drive his wife crazy by adjusting the gaslights in their London townhouse. The husband's strategy is simple: He continually denies his wife's observations that the lights in their house are changing. The assault on her mind pushes her to the brink of insanity by undermining her sense of reality and belief in her own senses.[2] Welch said that today's gaslighters work in the public square to create confusion and prey on public vulnerability, using sophisticated forms of manipulation, mind games and PR spin.

Welch, who is past chair of clinical psychology at the California Institute of Integral Studies, believes the Western mind is increasingly gullible because it is overwhelmed by too much information and rattled by fear about what's happening in our world and to our climate. In recent years, our minds have been faced with a steep learning curve. Demands on our brains have increased exponentially because of the rapid pace of change and all the information we must assimilate, respond to and grapple with. Welch said more and more people are less and less able to make sense of, and rationally adapt to, this alarming onslaught. When the mind is overloaded, "we engage in increasingly archaic, increasingly primitive forms of mental solutions," which include wishful thinking, denial and turning away from unpleasant stimuli.[3]

When the mind is in a "state of collapse," we also turn to others to lead us, people who are attractive and hold strong opinions. Simple answers are less taxing for us to absorb, especially when we're faced with a complex issue such as climate change, Welch said. An authoritative person who takes command—"think of Fox News or Rush Limbaugh"—and spews strong feelings with absolute certainty is appealing to a beleaguered mind.

The darker side of public relations thrives on this legitimate longing for clarity. Welch said people today have become vulnerable to an "absolutist situation...a rationalization for doing away with the sacrifices needed to confront a problem" such as climate change. The choice is not easy when one person warns, "We're going to lose our planet" and another argues, "Not true; you don't have to confront that horrible possibility." When the first expert is painted as an elitist, "fuzzy intellectual," it's even easier to tune them out and turn toward "maladaptive kinds of mechanisms."

Today's assault on experts is combined with a new attitude that encourages people to believe whatever feels better, Welch suggested. Comedian Stephen Colbert joked about this trend in 2006: "Who's *Britannica* to tell me that the Panama Canal was built in 1914? If I want to say that it was built in 1941, that's my right as an American."[4] Welch explained this mindset drives many primitive political processes. "It's what you see with the Tea Party group." Once you begin to eliminate supports for rational thinking and actively encourage

**When people hear the same message,
in the same language, over and over again,
it functions like an implant.**

BRYANT WELCH

people to indulge in beliefs that make them feel good, it's a downward slope. "People are drinking Kool-Aid," Welch commented.

Bryant Welch called this process of manipulation gaslighting because people begin to doubt their own perceptions and observations. When that happens, their autonomy is eroded and they become dependent upon those who foist their own versions of reality on others. People become less rational, less capable of thinking for themselves, "more and more beholden to Fox News." Welch noted that many people are now reliant upon a strong, forceful person telling them what to think.

He sees "gaslighting" examples everywhere: in mass communications, in the Iraq war, in the reaction to 9/11 and in climate change. He sees legitimate scientists describing how climate is changing, while ideologically oriented groups—such as the Competitive Enterprise Institute, the CATO Institute, and the Heartland Institute— confuse people and reconstruct a different "scientific reality."

It's conscious, it's deliberate, and it is becoming an art form in government, said Welch, who spent the first part of his career in private psychotherapy practice and later worked for the American Psychological Association in Washington. He was struck by the contrast: In individual practice the dialogue involves people struggling to be totally honest and see reality as clearly as possible. In the public dialogue in Washington, Welch found the opposite: people trying to weave a whole new reality. Welch called this a Rovian approach[5] of fraudulent spin: "Let's see if we can convince people that John Kerry is unfit to lead. What's the guy's strongest point? His military service.... So we simply start telling people that Kerry was a coward unfit to lead—and then you create that reality." The technique starts from a false point of view and manipulates other people to revise their reality.

Welch says it's propaganda, pure and simple—but why are we susceptible to lies or misinformation? Like a microchip implanted in a person's brain, the effectiveness of propaganda grows with constant repetition. American political satirist Jon Stewart occasionally runs a series of news excerpts showing a dozen or more talking heads from an administration—all of them spouting the identical language about an issue. As people hear the same language over and over, it functions like an implant. When you give a little chip to a mind that is struggling to come up with answers, the mind is grateful because it doesn't like to look stupid. People don't want to appear overwhelmed or confused, so they welcome the implant. It's easier than having to collect information, listen to differing points of view, talk to experts, read and make a decision.

People today cannot tolerate a state of uncertainty and anxiety. "The country's terrified. People are terrified," said the therapist. The less people can think for themselves the more frightened they become; this is exacerbated by the pace of change. Yet as US President Franklin Roosevelt said, "The only thing to fear is fear itself."[6]

Bryant Welch believes that antidotes to fear lie in the wisdom of the ancients, "A lot of the contemplative practices from the east— meditation, yoga—are tremendously effective in treating trauma." If people were more centered in their own experience in the present, with less grasping and agitation, we would see a calmer and less gullible population.

Welch also said that the best response to gaslighting is awareness. Expose the manipulation, just like in the movie—when the Scotland Yard detective reveals what has been happening to the wife. Her autonomy is restored the moment she recognizes how her husband has manipulated her.

I asked Welch what happens on a national scale when political leaders use gaslighting to manipulate reality; he said it creates a dynamic very similar to that which existed between the husband and wife in *Gaslight*. At first, people are confused by the false reality. Then they doubt their own senses, become more and more dependent, more invested in bigger and more outrageous lies: "We're going into Iraq because he has weapons of mass destruction." Or, "It's because he was part of Al-Qaeda." Or, "Maybe he's just developing weapons of mass destruction" or maybe Canada's sovereignty is being attacked by foreign-funded radicals. It changes by the month, and people end up not being able to think for themselves.

13

Summary:
The Polluted Public Square

A Personal Story

When I was seven years old my friend Donnie Fisherman and I used to go to a park and play in an old dirt cave that stretched deep into the side of a hill. It had a small entrance, a little chimney exit in the roof at the back and it was dark, spooky and exciting.

One day we were playing there, and a gang of bigger boys came along with boards and plywood and closed off the entrances. Donnie and I panicked in the damp, earthy blackness, and the more scared we became, the more we yelled and screamed, the more this gang of toughs laughed and taunted us.

It was my first experience with bullying, but it wasn't the last, because I grew up in a rough part of Calgary, Alberta, in Canada. I ran into violence not only going to and from school but also at home because my dad was an unpredictable, violent man who used to thrash the hell out of me and my mother. One time, when my mother was in hospital having trouble with a pregnancy, my father decided to give me a haircut, and he told me that if my mother died it would be my fault. He went into a crazy rage and hit me with the razor. I still have a scar on the side of my face. I was a good athlete at school, and my high jumping ability came in handy that night when my father chased me into the backyard. Energized by terror, I vaulted over the high back fence and flew down the lane.

These experiences didn't crush me. I fought back. I didn't want to be a wimp, and as time went by I too meted out some rough justice. I turned into a scrapper, got into fights, became friends with some very tough guys and sometimes slipped into bullying.

But as I grew older I began to learn a pivotal life lesson—about the fine line between standing up against bullies and becoming a bully yourself.

My teenage years were confusing. I grew up with stories of the Lone Ranger and John Wayne riding around in my head, and those romantic narratives told me that the good guys were right and justice prevailed. My own decisions to fight back didn't always unfold in such a heroic way, however, and in real life things were not so clear cut: Good guys could be bad, and bad guys could be good. Sometimes the good guy got a black eye, a bloody nose and a fat lip. Sure, sometimes when I was fighting back I was the good guy standing up for myself, but other times I was just a bully pushing around someone who couldn't really fight back. Now and then I was the coward who didn't want to fight. Fighting back wasn't always a story about courage and right triumphing over wrong.

A lot of people spiral downward because of abuse or bullying, but I was incredibly fortunate to become interested in meditation, Eastern philosophy and Buddhism. In the 1960s I fell in with a group of people interested in Eastern thought—from Zen philosophy and mysticism to Gandhi—and I turned in a new direction. I began reading Alan Watts and Aldous Huxley, and started going out with a young woman who was into Buddhism, a flower child. It was the '60s after all, a time of peace and love, and I realized that being a minor gangster was not cool.

Years later, after graduating from law school, I built a successful PR firm specializing in crisis and issues management, where I helped clients navigate through public controversy, difficult reputational problems and acrimonious court cases. From time to time, I ran across PR aggressors and intimidators, people who didn't know where to draw the line, who played fast and loose with the truth. These raw attempts to threaten and browbeat riled me, but it was on a small scale compared with what was to come.

At one time I naïvely believed that transparency was the answer. I thought that if you turned on the lights the cockroaches would scuttle back into the corners. Then I got involved in the David Suzuki Foundation and found out that sometimes when you turn on the lights the cockroaches just get bigger, meaner and more aggressive. When I stepped into the environmental arena a new world opened up to me, rife with muscular propaganda and PR pressure that was shockingly worse than anything I'd ever imagined. Discussions about climate change, energy consumption and the destruction of ecosystems seemed to trigger an ideological craziness that resulted in wild escalations of rhetoric and extreme polarization.

I found the attacks on scientists and the volume of propaganda used to cloud environmental issues puzzling. I found myself becoming angrier about the deception and lack of fair play than I was about environmental damage itself. I wondered why, then one day it hit me: Bullies aren't just a problem in the schoolyard. They also try to take your lunch money and intimidate you in the public square.

Moving Into the Square

When it comes to the environment, the public square is thick with bullies who want to protect their interests or assert their ideology with indifference. Just like the boys outside that dirt cave, they try to dominate others; I was angered about the attitude of people who feel it's okay to behave like this.

The foreign-funded radicals campaign in Canada was about bullying and demonizing. Climategate was the same, an attempt to malign scientists and disparage their work. When American marine biologist and conservationist Rachel Carson raised concerns about the health dangers of pesticides in her 1962 book *Silent Spring*, she was called an hysterical woman, a communist and a radical.[1] Such attacks are never intended to be part of a legitimate debate. These are all attempts to shut people up—and bullying has always been at the heart of propaganda.

A core question—considering the insights and warnings from Kahan, Tavris, Conner and Haidt about being careful not to make matters worse—is how to communicate in a way that is more accessible to more people, regardless of their values or politics. How can we stand up for what is right and against what is wrong, without becoming bullies ourselves?

As American linguist Deborah Tannen said, our argumentative culture is endangering our civic life because "when there's a ruckus in the street outside your home, you fling open the window to see what's happening. But if there's a row outside every night, you shut the window and try to block it out."[2]

There has long been a difference of opinion about how to advocate. Some suggest aggressive outspoken advocacy is needed while others prefer working with opponents and finding common ground. It's no surprise these issues have sparked many a debate at Suzuki Foundation board meetings. Even civil rights leaders such as Martin Luther King and Mahatma Gandhi had to defend themselves when followers questioned the effectiveness of nonviolent resistance.

My own experience fighting bullies in the rough-and-tumble world of PR has taught me these key strategies:

1. Be slow to pick public fights because fighting fire with fire seldom settles a dispute or issue in your favor. I have often told clients, who wanted to weigh in on a front-page controversy, to heed the warning of George Bernard Shaw, who said, "I learned long ago, never to wrestle with a pig. You get dirty, and besides, the pig likes it." I usually add my own clarification, which is, after a while people can't tell the difference between you and the pig.

2. If you don't tell your own story, someone else will—and it will be bad. Not telling your own story is like not showing up for the game: You lose by default.

These can be contradictory pieces of advice: One tells you to step into the media spotlight and stand up for what you think; the other says don't react. But either strategy may be valid, depending on the situation.

The more I ponder David Suzuki's question about why we are failing to act, despite the warnings of scientists about looming environmental catastrophes, the more I realize we need to become much more savvy about the environment of public debate, so we don't slip into perpetual antagonism, anger and confusion. How do we communicate in a more persuasive and less polarizing, alienating and enflaming manner? And how do we navigate between strong, honest debate and the kind of narrative that drives us further into entrenched, defensive positions?

At its heart, *I'm Right* is about miscommunication resulting from narrative failure on the part of advocates. This has opened the floodgates to industry propaganda and polarization from all sides — whether from government, vested interests or environmental advocates — and miscommunication has created pollution in the public square, whether intentional or not. The results have been gridlock and shuttered windows.

It's a difficult balancing act, but we want to walk a fine line between speaking out against what is wrong and avoiding the advocacy trap.

New Directions for Advocates

If we truly believe that "the sky is falling"—and the vast majority of climate scientists say it is—we ought to be willing to question how we engage around this issue and learn to communicate better.

I hope that *I'm Right* will guide other communicators in government, industry and civil society who feel they are up against a rock wall. So this book is written for right-thinking people, on any side of these difficult issues, who care about what happens in their community and have an opportunity to influence the course of events.

It may help people reconsider what they are doing or, for those not yet involved who may be wringing their hands and wanting to do something, it may help them be successful.

We've learned about powerful psychological and social forces—part of the human condition—that cause us to line up in self-righteous teams and be blind to other points of view, and we've learned how unbelievably powerful it feels to believe we are on the side of Right, and to brand opposition as wrongdoers. But I can't help thinking it would be wiser to keep in mind, as Carol Tavris and others reminded me, that we could be wrong.

We have learned how the advocacy trap stirs up anger, and how we stop thinking clearly when we treat those who disagree with us as enemies. This drives people away from solutions and understanding. DeSmogBlog started there, and it took me a while to realize that attacking people's motives and intentions, even if they seem suspect, fuels their resistance as well as the resistance of people who believe them. Sometimes it's necessary, but it can lead to gridlock and despair—which is the opposite of what those seeking climate solutions want. Even lawyers, duking it out in court, struggle to refer to each other as "my good colleague" or "my learned friend," and the older we get, the more we realize our parents taught us about civility for a reason.

Bryant Welch believes that nonviolent speech is effective because a lack of response from someone who is attacked undercuts "the projective devices that adversaries use to justify their aggression." If the victim remains silent, it is much harder for an aggressor to sustain an attack, because "the perpetrator is left to stew in his or her own ugly juices. They are slowed in their attempts at self-justification," Welch explained.[3]

When I was in London, doing early research for this book, I interviewed Baroness Onora O'Neill at the House of Lords. The British philosopher is a graduate of Oxford and Harvard, has written extensively about the importance of respect for autonomy and trust, and suggests we "need to free professionals and the public service to serve the public…to work towards more intelligent forms of accountability…and to rethink a media culture in which spreading suspicion has become a routine activity."[4]

O'Neill chairs the Equality and Human Rights Commission, which is responsible for the enforcement of equity and non-discrimination laws in Great Britain.[5] She told me it is important for people to understand the difference between information and public relations, especially PR that gets carried away. She further suggested that journalists should be talking to "competent scientists as opposed to non-competent scientists"[6] and fraudsters. The public, meanwhile, should be educated to better understand what it means when a scientific paper is described as peer reviewed.

In the past few decades, O'Neill said, the public relations industry has led us to "re-conceptualize trust as an attitude rather than a judgment." Advertising bumf and PR fluff that focus on attitudes is fine when you are buying cereal or a sofa but not when buying into climate change denial, she said. This is when we need to use our discrimination to make a sound judgment.

"There is well-placed trust that is badly placed…and there is badly placed mistrust where a person mistrusts the trustworthy." O'Neill explained that we need to turn this around and start trusting the trustworthy and mistrusting the untrustworthy. What we typically see today is a denial of the relevance of expertise because we're led to believe that everybody's opinion is as good as anybody else's.

Baroness O'Neill noted it is increasingly difficult to judge which people or which institutions to trust because we live in "a complex society where a great deal of communication is mediated. If I lived in a village of 30 or 50 years ago I would have a sense of who was telling tall tales. I would have people in context," but today it's a different story. So how do we find the truth in this new world? "You don't get it by looking at attitudes. You get it by making a complex judgment… in a combination of competence, honesty and reliability. You have to have evidence; you have to know a person's track record, whether he has anything at stake, what other people think of him. You wouldn't just have an attitude."

In recent years, said O'Neill, we have shifted from a state where "civil servants had integrity and did their jobs, and politicians did their job and courts did theirs." We now have powerful media pumping out misinformation or partial information, and a lot of journalists offering "regurgitations of press releases because they don't have time or knowledge to do anything more." We also live in a culture where so-called news is more about sports figures and celebrities than real issues. She said we are witnessing "a celebration of denial and the maintenance of a destructive way of life."

During this research, I developed a new perspective on polarization from a 2013 PBS special in which Bill Moyers and Harvard University social justice advocate Marshall Ganz discussed the power of social movements and how to achieve meaningful change. Ganz told viewers to never be afraid of controversy. He has no time for people who criticize polarization and say "Let's all just get along better." Ganz said we need more polarization, not less.[7] What? I yelled out loud. I was so shocked that I phoned him right away, but after a short conversation I started to understand the difference between polarization and what I would call bullying.

Never shy away from an important argument or fear taking a combative stance, Ganz stressed when I spoke with him.[8] "This idea that contentiousness is somehow alien to democracy, that consensus is somehow what democracy is about and that polarization is bad—is all wrong. We are really screwed up on that.... Paralysis is what's bad," explained the veteran activist. Polarization is a necessary precursor to negotiation, and our systems of decision-making should encourage more debate and controversy, not less. "Organizers have to be willing to be schizoids, because they have to polarize to mobilize, and then depolarize to settle." Without polarization and opposition, people never mobilize.

He said Obama made a huge tactical error in 2012 with his "shocking passivity" in the first presidential debate against Mitt Romney. Although seemingly rooted in the President's view that good leadership should rise above the petty bickering, such a conciliatory stance is not only an instrumental problem but a moral problem, "severely compromising the adversarial mechanisms that the citizenry must rely on to bring out the truth." Ganz said Obama had a responsibility to argue in the pursuit of truth, just as the prosecution or defense lawyer in a criminal case should never avoid argument, as that would undermine the entire function of adversarial litigation. His strategy of trying to sound like a statesman and elevate himself above the argument backfired.

Ganz added many of his students slip into conflict avoidance too often and too easily. They have a mistaken idea that if everyone talks things out, everyone will eventually agree and we can all move forward with consensus. Ganz argues that consensus is what you get in an authoritarian regime, not a healthy democracy where citizens are free to challenge injustice. But he was quick to note that debate, when used for reasons of power rather than truth, leads to gridlock in the halls of government. So while he believes contention lies at the heart of democracy, it must be constructive contention.

Ganz explained we should make sure that our argument is an "argument for the sake of heaven," as described by Hillel and Panim in an early commentary on the Jewish Torah.[9] An argument for the sake of heaven aims to counteract injustice and bring out truth, not to defeat an opponent. Its goal is not focused on winning, crushing someone or grasping at power. In an argument for the sake of heaven each side listens willingly and seriously to others' views and analyzes points using reason and respect. We will never solve problems such as climate change if we don't join discussions, and if we sit on the sidelines our children's futures will be lost—but we need to be respectful of other human beings and not attack them or their opinions.

Communication is an art, not a science, and we all learn in the doing. At its most basic level, *I'm Right* is about how we tell stories and how we treat each other. The best stories are iterative and interactive; they grow in the telling, and when they are powerful and compelling they can withstand a maelstrom of negative PR spin. By telling inclusive stories that are well-crafted and relate to who we are, that help us and others understand the world around us, we can counter pollution in the public square. We also have a responsibility to our own narratives, to keep our own minds open and to seek to expand the minds of others.

This doesn't mean giving up on our principles or becoming wimps, but it does mean avoiding the unintended quicksand of anger-charged messages that drag us all down. The most effective stories enlighten and integrate; they're not selfish, greedy or abusive. We don't want to turn a right-versus-wrong narrative into a perpetual us-versus-them story that increases the amplitude of the opposition. Can we think of more culturally accessible ways to take on destructive propaganda, beliefs and values? Yes. And the rest of this book explores how we might argue for the sake of heaven.

PART II

Speak the Truth,
But Not to Punish

In this part of *I'm Right* we consider how to clean up our polluted public square. Through the eyes of some of the world's great public intellectuals, we learn how to move beyond the one-sided rhetoric, warlike opposition and the *ad hominem* attacks that create toxic discourse.

We investigate the attitudes, knowledge and skills that can take public conversations to a deeper level, so that we can actually change people's minds about what's desirable and what's possible.

We look at how to communicate more effectively and disagree more constructively, using the language of emotions and deep values. Some people will be forever locked into their opinions, but for most others it is possible to have an authentic, mind-changing conversation.

Leaning
Into the Future

14

Power and Love

with ADAM KAHANE

CANADIAN FACILITATOR Adam Kahane is an authority on social change and has spent much of his career outside Canada, working to find creative, durable solutions for some of the world's toughest problems. After starting his career in the 1980s at Royal Dutch Shell (a world leader in scenario planning), he co-founded Reos Partners and has since traveled the globe, helping resolve everything from thorny environmental, political and economic problems to issues of nutrition, energy and security—much of it through an advanced and specialized form of dialogue called Scenario Planning. Kahane is the author of several books about his methods.[1]

One of Adam Kahane's first high-profile successes was in 1991–92, just as apartheid was ending in South Africa and Nelson Mandela had been released from prison. At this crucial time, Kahane facilitated the Mont Fleur Scenario Exercises, in which a diverse group of 22 leaders from across the ideological spectrum of South African society worked together to construct possible narratives about the future of their country. In the midst of great conflict and mistrust, this innovative and important project enabled him to work with South African politicians, business people, trade unionists, academics and activists—black and white—to establish a common vocabulary and mutual understanding for moving into the future.

Kahane enabled people to set aside their personal, political and business biases so they could discuss possibilities, and these exercises were part of many dialogues and negotiations that helped a new political landscape evolve.

Trevor Manuel, who chaired South Africa's National Planning Commission said, "Every leader, policymaker, and citizen can learn and take strength from Kahane's central message: By working together, setting aside prejudices, and developing trust, we can change the future." Similar accolades came from Colombian president Juan Manuel Santos: "Sixteen years ago Adam Kahane came to Colombia and worked with us on the future of our country. The four scenarios we built back then have come to life, one after another, and today we are living the best."[2]

With his immense knowledge and experience I knew Kahane was someone I should talk to about the current state of public discourse. Yet Kahane's experience in more than 50 countries around the globe did not prepare him for what is happening now in his native country. "I'm surprised at the polarization," he said. "I could say, worse than that, the demonization of public discourse generally, but especially around environment issues. We see this in many countries on many issues, but I was expecting something better in Canada."[3] And as people protest around pipelines, Kahane noted that he is witnessing levels of fragmentation, polarization, and demonization almost as dramatic as those he's seen in other countries.

"In particular, this controversy over the so-called foreign funding of NGOs is extraordinary. I mean there are lots of countries that don't like foreign funding of NGOs—Russia, Uganda—but it's not normally an issue in the West." Kahane was also shocked by the delegitimization of opponents on both sides during the Harper years. "I've been surprised at the extent to which the people who work on climate change consider the elected majority government to be beyond the pale and impossible to engage with.... It's mutual demonization."

Kahane went on to explain that many issues can be successfully

**The tension between power and love
is at the very center of all social change work.**

ADAM KAHANE

addressed only through collaborative, co-created work by actors from government, business and civil society.

Adam Kahane's work has shown him it is increasingly vital for people to work together, not just with friends and colleagues, but also with strangers and opponents, even enemies, in order to address knotty challenges, of which climate change is an extreme example. How do we get people to the table, and what should we do when we're there? First, he doesn't spend any energy trying to convince people to do something they don't want to. He looks instead for an attitude—whether from NGOs, corporations or governments—a shift that shows people finally recognize they cannot get where they want to alone. They are ready to come together because "usually they have bumped their head hard."

Kahane stressed that people need not agree on a vision in order to start working together. "The common theme in all our work is helping teams of actors from across different organizations and sectors who all think that something needs to be done in their system. They don't need to agree on the solution or on the problem. They don't need to understand each other, trust each other or even like each other." But they do have to recognize that the only way to move forward is together.

If actors are not initially willing to participate, he tries to find a way in, a crack. Even simply agreeing that the situation is dire can sometimes be enough of a toehold that will allow the actors to begin to engage with one another. He described this kind of work as a perpetual cycle that alternates between advocating and collaborating, "between pushing with all your strength for what you believe is true and right, and sitting and talking, trying to work with people who you don't understand, or trust, or like." The stress of going from the ramparts to the negotiating table is exacerbated by power imbalances—the power of money, or politics or ideas, Kahane said.

Adam Kahane calls the two basic pillars of his work power and love. Most people associate the word power with oppression and love with romance, but Kahane quotes theologian Paul Tillich who said power is the drive of everything living to realize itself with increasing intensity and extensity, and love is the drive to unify the separated.[4] "The tension between power and love is at the very center of all social change work," said Kahane.

Both love and power have a generative and a degenerative side when taken to extremes. For instance, nothing happens without power, without an engine to drive us forward. But when taken too far, power becomes a destructive and confrontational steamroller. Similarly, love can engender a sense of oneness and collaboration but can also be suffocating and emasculating. Kahane quoted Martin Luther King: "Power without love is reckless and abusive, and love without power is sentimental and anemic."[5]

Coming unstuck requires knowing when to exercise both power and love, and Kahane noted that the elegance of this model applies at any scale of social system, from a family to a global issue.

He described a meeting he once had with a deputy minister who said, "We need a method for working on stuck files." This intrigued Kahane because whether you are working in Ottawa or Washington, there are certain things you can't make progress on. You keep pushing, but can't move forward. Why? Because no single institution, even one as large as a federal government, can successfully address many of today's difficult problems. He recalled the beginnings of this in Ottawa 20 years ago when another deputy minister pointed out, "We've been trained to think that we can fix or deal with societal issues by pulling these levers, and we've discovered that these levers are not attached to anything."

Kahane noted that humanity is increasingly stuck in complex and polarized situations for three reasons:

1. We cannot solve the really tough problems by working only on our little piece.
2. We cannot transform large systems by working only with people we like, with our friends and colleagues.
3. We must learn to work with strangers and opponents, people we don't know or trust or agree with. Without this simple awareness we will have gridlock.

One of the most effective ways to get unstuck is to tell stories that enable us to create new futures, hence Kahane's focus on transformational scenarios. These scenarios are not forecasts about what could or should happen. They are not attempts to make predictions or blueprints, or to come up with solutions. They are designed to generate new thinking about the future. "They are not about what people want, but about what's possible."

In the Mont Fleur process, each scenario was named for a bird. The Ostrich stuck its head in the sand, so problems festered; the Lame Duck represented a new government, but with so many restrictions it never got off the ground; Icarus embodied the idea of elation and freedom, but ignored fiscal constraints and crashed the economy; but the Flamingo symbolized gradual rebuilding and flight as a group.

Kahane explained that transformative scenario planning contains a crucial paradox: Those involved become very creative when they have to be absolutely objective and think deeply about fashioning a new situation. The actors do not have to understand, agree, or trust each other in order to work constructively and openly in the creation of new stories, but they do have to agree that the scenarios they envision could actually happen.

Kahane explained that his methodology involves five simple steps:

1. An organizer convenes a team from across the whole system in question.
2. The team observes what is happening in the system

3. The team constructs stories about what could happen
4. The team discovers from these stories what can and must be done
5. The team then takes action to transform the system.

Although simple, it is not easy, Kahane explained, because the actors typically have strong and opposing feelings, opinions and emotions. In addition, this kind of emergent process is unpredictable, uncontrollable or uncomfortable. Participants have to accept that some things will never change. This can be difficult. The first step is to just gather the actors together with a common goal, "not to take action, but to try to understand what is possible.... It's a much lower bar for participation."

How does Adam Kahane encourage people to work together? He believes that two things generate movement toward resolution: a feeling of frustration and a deep desire for change. "If I could get there alone why would I bother to sit in long meetings with people I don't trust and don't agree with?" Is dialogue, by itself, sufficient? "The answer is sometimes yes but more often no. Dialogue alone does not advance a problematic situation because we need to change not only what we're saying, but also what we're doing. That's a challenge for people who hope a pressing problem will go away by just talking about it. That's one reason why working in Canada can be so difficult: the status quo works just fine for most people and is a significant barrier to change." Whereas the advantage of working in South Africa or Guatemala or India is that "nobody has any illusion that things are just fine the way they are."

Kahane said the time limit associated with climate change is what makes it exceptional—and exceptionally difficult. We need creative work to get out of the climate change box because it is an extremely serious challenge; it has been the most clearly explained future crisis ever, and yet even that much information has failed to motivate people, he noted.

I suggested that industry and the Harper government might have done a better job of managing their interests if they decided to be less combative and more constructive. He agreed and pointed out there were opportunities to be seized and costs to be lessened through engagement: "But there was a basic problem here that couldn't just be wished away through hand waving. What's surprising to me is that the dangers and costs of climate change were not taken more seriously by the population at large and by the Harper government in particular." Yes, there were major costs associated with change, but the price of not changing is to live in an over-heated world: "I don't get why those slightly longer-term questions could not be grasped." People tend to say, "Yeah, yeah, yeah. The world's burning, but…we're not going to fix this on the back of my stockholders, my employees, my tax bill." He was amazed that we made so little progress, and in some areas were backsliding. "It's willful denial of the effects we're already feeling."

I asked if he believed Canada's federal government of the day (Harper's Conservatives) and industry had chosen this kind of combative style because the alternative was too damaging to business. Kahane agreed that it did seem that provincial and federal governments were saying the costs of addressing environmental concerns—not just for companies, but also for tax revenues and national economic production—are too high. "We are simply not willing to sacrifice immediate benefits for an unpredictable future benefit. I don't think it's any more complicated than that."

Is Adam Kahane hopeful we can make progress on the climate file? Not until the cost of failing to engage with these issues and in collaborative action—for companies, governments, the voting public and consumers—is so high that ignoring it is no longer feasible.

Kahane explained one of the biggest, longest-standing and most successful multi-stakeholder, dialogue-in-action projects he has ever been involved with is the Sustainable Food Lab. He was the co-initiator of the project (with Hal Hamilton), and in 2004 during the first round of recruitment interviews he had an interesting insight while meeting with the head of one NGO. Kahane's group listened very carefully during several days at the organizer's farm, but at the end of the meetings the man stated flatly: "Look, it's very clear what you want to do, but I am actually not interested in entering into dialogue with these corporations until I'm stronger and they take me seriously."

Kahane suggested that this is why environmental activism is absolutely critical to advance dialogue and may have to be scaled up tenfold before it has the necessary impact on businesses and governments. Even when dialogue does start, don't give up on mobilizing voters, consumers and protesters, he advised. You want to keep the pressure up, because people are never keen to act against their immediate interests. We all hear statements like: "Let's just put our interests and agendas aside and talk about what's best for the world." This is nonsensical, a ridiculous request of individuals, companies or governments. He noted it's equivalent to saying, "Why don't you stop breathing while you're in this room?"

Kahane returned to his earlier theme about power and love: These two seemingly contradictory forces have much to teach us about the state of public discourse in the world today, whether a debate revolves around food security, judicial reform or climate change. Power helps us get the job done, achieve our ambitions. "Without it, nothing, literally nothing, would happen in the world," Kahane said, adding that the ambition of politicians, oil companies and activists is all part of that power. Love becomes a critical counterbalance because power without love means everyone is doing their own thing, pushing for what they alone want. It's a scenario that's all about individual self-interest and ambition, without any recognition of the impact these might have on others, or society as a whole. Climate change is the ultimate example of this.

Kahane explained that pollution in the public square happens when one factor is applied without the tempering influence of the other: People exercise power without love by driving enormous cars or wasting resources in ways that are "ultimately destroying the conditions for life on the planet." But the opposite is equally important, perhaps more so. Love without power pays attention only to the good of the whole, what's best for humanity, and denies or ignores the interests and drives of the parts.

The best way to navigate is by paying attention to both power and love. It's like walking on two legs, he said, adding that without dynamically balancing and shifting from one to the other, we cannot propel ourselves and society forward—whether we're working with executives, political leaders, activists or guerillas.

Understanding the anatomy of a problem like climate change is helpful, and Kahane outlined three dimensions at play:

1. Dynamic Complexity—cause and effect are far apart in space and time, yet interdependent. For example the coal we burned 50 years ago is influencing our climate today, or oil sands in Alberta are affecting rainfall in South Africa.
2. Social Complexity—the actors have fundamentally different perspectives, interests and worldviews.
3. Generative Complexity—situations are fundamentally unfamiliar and unpredictable. For instance, "We can't do what we did last time we heated up the planet like this."

For reasons that are pretty obvious when looking at these three dimensions, climate change is, in most respects, the most difficult problem in the world, Kahane said and that's why, in spite of enormous, serious, intelligent, good-willed efforts, we are not making progress.

But by engaging with varied groups—people who are not like us, who operate in other parts of the system—we can begin to look at things differently. We can see things we may not have seen before, things we may not have wanted to see. It helps us overcome stereotypes and recognize how we might do things differently—although it doesn't always prompt us to do things differently. Studies have shown that the elites understand the climate change problem best, but that doesn't reduce their airplane trips to climate change conferences or their overseas holidays. Which is why we need countervailing pressures.

High-quality communication is critical, and that springs from open-mindedness, self-awareness and good listening skills. Kahane said good communication is not simply downloading our own view. As long as we are stuck in downloading mode, we are impervious to change, Kahane explained. The first step is to suspend our story, "to hang it on a string in front of us, put that little bit of distance between me and my story." This allows us to see it, question it and maybe at the end of the conversation, take it back and say, "I think that story is really not effective, or accurate or appropriate anymore."

The act of suspending says, "I am open to the possibility of changing, but if others don't also take that step we remain stuck parroting our set speeches to each other," which by the way, probably occupies 80 to 90 percent of usual discourse.

Kahane was working in Zimbabwe recently, in a highly charged, violently polarized political and social system, and the one thing that stuck with people at the end of the session was the word *suspending*; this pleased Kahane greatly because if you can remember only one word, that's the most important lesson from your experience. Suspending doesn't mean I'm rejecting my position or story, but I am making myself aware of it and making you aware of it, and giving us both permission to question it, to even attack it, without attacking me.

As powerful as dialogue is, Kahane said it would be a fundamental error to focus on that alone. "It's certainly part of the story, but dialogue is, above all, a love methodology, a love tool for uniting the separated. I'm all for love tools," but once again, love without power is dialogue without connection to action and implementation. "I have devoted my life to dialogue. I think there's a lot to be said for it, but the answer is not to scale up dialogue alone but to connect the dialogue with action to effect systemic change." Kahane warned that love without power is more dangerous than power without love because it's hidden. "It produces perverted outcomes. Be careful of trying to walk on one leg."

I mentioned to Kahane that it's impossible to discount the persuasive power of some of the great leaders in history, who weren't involved in dialogue at all but single-mindedly focused on persuasion. He took that point further, explaining that the important dichotomy is not between dialogue and persuasion but between dialogue and unilateral action. Kahane argued that both are required. Things change in the world when people see something that needs to be done and something that is, in some sense, in their interests. So they act accordingly. They may act insensitively, forcefully and in some cases even violently, but without that kind of drive many things would not take shape.

The dangers involved in pure power without love, however, are rampant and are leading to the destruction of our planet, he said. "We mustn't let the pendulum swing to one side or the other."

15

No Fish? No Fish Sticks

with PETER SENGE

PETER SENGE[1] is a world leader in systems thinking, and when helping students understand what he means by systems, Senge asks if they have ever seen how members of families sometimes produce unintentional consequences through their actions or feelings. This helps students step outside the world of theoretical jargon and into the reality that we all live in webs of interdependence. It's also a view of systems thinking that helps everyone gain a perspective on the "vexing, difficult and intransigent" problems we deal with, not to mention "some leverage and insight as to what we might do differently."[2]

I wanted to know why we are ignoring the alarm bells that scientists are ringing about environmental crises, and why we are bogged down by acrid debate. Senge is skeptical about debates in general and said universities are great places for people to argue round and round a topic, but these exercises usually achieve little. Senge explained that a key reason why debate falls short in global warming discussions is that scientists are excellent at forming new questions and discovering new areas of uncertainty but not particularly good at producing consensus around complex issues. Climate change is an iconic example of this failing, and, "the climate science community has done a poor job of helping the public understand even the most basic ideas about which there is a very broad consensus."

For example, a simple fact of climate science is that greenhouse gas emissions accumulate in the atmosphere and that, consequently, reducing emissions will not reduce GHG concentration until emissions are reduced to below the rate at which GHG are removed from the atmosphere (e.g., via natural sequestration). Not understanding this rudimentary climate bathtub concept leads many lay people to never intuitively understand why massive reductions (80 percent or more) in emissions will be needed—and that consequently we inevitably face long delays in solving this problem. Widespread misunderstanding of this basic concept also makes the "wait until we are all certain" strategy exactly the wrong strategy.

Science is basically organized around communities of enquiry that investigate smaller questions within much larger fields. Scientists typically produce deep knowledge about pieces, elements or aspects of a complex system such as climate change, but not Earth's climate system itself. So, when dealing with truly interdependent issues, mainstream science is often dysfunctional. Also, asking scientists what they all agree on is a waste of time because science never does, nor should, produce unanimity. Scientists are naturally focused on challenging existing ideas and sharpening debates that can illuminate future questions.

Society is faced with a two-fold problem: Not only do scientists have difficulty communicating intuitively and effectively, but also the environmental community is "addicted to a fear-based strategy, hammering away at how awful everything is, so not surprisingly this leads a lot of people to just tune out."

We need to put the puzzle pieces together and look at group problem solving using systems thinking, Senge said flatly, because "reality is made up of circles, and we see straight lines."

A systems thinking approach has three characteristics:
1. A deep and abiding commitment to real learning
2. An ability to admit that we too are part of the problem
3. The ability to triangulate, to gather different points of view from people in different parts of the system, so we can see something more holistically that is eluding us individually.

**Every single problem is a subset
of this mega problem of not being able to understand
the complexity that we have created.**

PETER SENGE

Senge also described the need for collective intelligence, not simply individual intelligence. When we pool our best ideas and work cooperatively, we end up with cities that operate differently, industrial sectors that value change and produce social, ecological and economic well-being.

Senge's fascination with systems began at a young age. Something he realized even before attending college was that the "level of interdependence mankind has created in the world has vastly outstripped our ability to manage and understand that interdependence." He sees this challenge in every large and stubborn problem we face today, from environmental issues, to social concerns and global economics. "Every single problem is a subset of this mega problem of not being able to understand the complexity that we have created." Growing up in Los Angeles, Senge witnessed first-hand the completely out-of-control nature of urbanization: "[When I was] a child you could drive for miles and see nothing but orange and lemon groves, but within 10 years, they were gone, replaced by shopping malls and freeways. It was an astounding example of poorly considered sprawl, that created all kinds of unintended social, environmental, economic problems—and it had a big impact on me."

Senge saw the world around him as a total free-for-all where nothing was planned and everything was opportunistic. "It was driven by narrow economic interests and short term thinking, with consequences that would last for lifetimes." He compared urban sprawl to cancer, a simple growth process that spirals out of control when cells lose their sense of interdependence. Similar patterns of unrestrained expansion are now being played out all around the world.

I asked Senge about change resistance and the self-activating, balancing forces within systems that sustain them. Are they preventing us from fixing environmental problems, and if so how do we open up for change?

His answer was simple. On a biological level, one of the definitions of a living system is the ability to maintain balances crucial to survival. A living thing's first impulse is to maintain itself, and homoeostasis is the fundamental process creating that balance. In this sense, all systems resist change from the outside. If you push, the system will push back. We all know this at a personal level, Senge explained. "If someone says to you, 'Hey, Jim, be happy,' even though you might agree, you have a kind of a knee-jerk reaction to feel, 'Who are you to tell me to be happy?' So going around the world telling people what to think is a particularly bad idea, a bad change strategy."

We often forget this human trait, naïvely believing that the truth and logic of our argument will convince people to take action, but instead we trigger tendencies to dig in. He said it is important to understand this. "If you really think deeply about why things are the way they are, you see the forces conserving balances, and this knowledge can help shape more effective strategies."

And so, in any kind of change process, Senge advised that the initial strategy should be to start with inquiry and focus on where things are already moving. "It's the first rule of all learning: All learners learn what learners want to learn." When people are pushy and force us to learn something, it's off-putting. But if someone politely asks if you want to learn something, you might consider it. One of the reasons we forget this basic fact is that we all have our own values; when something is really important to us, we think it will be important to others, that they should learn it. "We forget it's the learner's values that matter, not ours. So the first question always has to do with motivation. What will genuinely motivate another person, organization or society?"

The next step is learning how to "follow the energy. Put your focus where things are headed in the right direction, rather than trying to stop a river that has been flowing in a certain direction for a very long time. There's an old saying in traditional Chinese culture: 'You cannot move the river; dig a new channel instead, and the river will move itself eventually.'"

Senge pointed out that we must always remember the unprecedented nature of global warming. We are being asked by science to surmount all of our history, personally and as a species, and believe that something that has never happened is now happening. So, it is not hard to grasp why underlying disbelief exists, and this disbelief is exactly what misinformation campaigns exploit. If people were predisposed to accept what evidence is showing, misinformation would likely not have the same hold that it does. We must remember that people holding this disbelief are not crazy. Since human-induced global climate change has never happened before, it is in some sense quite reasonable to question whether it could be happening now. Deep beliefs don't change quickly or easily. So focusing on convincing people who are anchored as climate contrarians is a low-level strategy. Peter Senge articulated a transcendent understanding in systemic change: "People don't necessarily resist change—but they do resist being changed."

"That's why I think it's a total waste of time to try and shift the political climate in Washington. I don't think it's a coincidence that there's aggressive leadership on climate change in Beijing and little in Washington." When leaders in Washington get overwhelmed, they revert to what they're most comfortable with "debating and acting lawyerly, because that's who they are." Most of the leaders in China, however, are engineers who want to get things done. Many understand the basic science of climate change, but of course they face their own very daunting problems, given the direction and inertia of the economic growth engine in China.[3]

Achieving change in the US will not be easy because entrenched interests are strong, whereas in China people are discovering incentives to accelerate an energy transition. "I find it's tragic that so few people outside China sense the forces trying to move in a different direction there. It's real." The Chinese Communist Party has aggressive targets for carbon intensity reduction of 40 to 45 percent this decade. "That's a really, really big deal and it's basically been ignored in the West. My personal feeling is that enough people in China, particularly in Beijing, have crossed the threshold...Their mindset has shifted and they are starting to believe that China can lead the energy transition, just as the West led the extraordinary shift to the fossil fuel economy. They have a different spirit and capability to confront really tough problems. It's state supported, and it's entrepreneurial."[4]

Senge believes the speed at which we are accomplishing change is woefully inadequate given the urgency of global climate change, but countries like Germany are also moving in the right direction, trying to accelerate decarbonization; other nations are strong on solar power. A major problem in the environmental movement in North America is the focus on convincing people of the problem and not accelerating entrepreneurial movement. Most large environmental NGOs are science based and have spent way too much energy trying to convince people of the science rather than supporting more rapid deployment of non-fossil fuel energy; promoting new energy sources is both environmentally sound and sound for the economy by virtue of the enterprises and employment it can create. More NGOs are starting to see that, "We need to find something that works, get out and do it. And do it again and again, and do it faster." We need to be more creative and proactive in scaling up much more rapidly. "We've got to make this feasible for millions and millions..."

Senge suggested that North Americans are stuck in a chicken-and-egg situation: The present policy environment is shaped by the political power of the coal-oil-gas-utility lobby, but activists play into their hands by making the argument about the environment, which simply is not a top-level political issue in the US. However, economic revitalization and employment, technological leadership and national security are issues that can move political consensus. The movement will not be easy because the status quo lobbies are so powerful, but those urging protection of environments need a sound political strategy.

Senge emphasized that systems thinking is very pragmatic. It tells us that change is motivated not by fighting resistance but by going where things are already moving, by finding high-leverage changes that can create an environment that is drifting in the desired direction. "You don't grow anything, even a single tree, by standing over a seedling and saying, 'It's a really good idea you should grow.' That's idiocy. You have to understand the water, nutrients and sunlight. You study the systems, the conditions, see where it is already growing and support that. If that innate growth process didn't exist, there would be nothing much you could do."

When applying this analogy to environmental advocacy, Senge said the first question is, Who is already trying to do something useful, and how do we support them? He believes fighting "wrongs" only gets us stuck in the past. We need to lean into the emerging future and work to accelerate positive efforts, and that means supporting companies that are aggressively doing the right things.

One example of potentially massive systems change thinking relates to the Internet, which currently consumes 8–10 percent of the world's electricity.[5] "That's a massive energy load, and it's been doubling worldwide every two or three years. Plus, people who see the Internet as pointing to our future believe technology is a key lever for change. Why not work toward a vision where the Internet is entirely based on alternative energy? You could start with huge server farms. Then concentrate on cell towers. Then, gradually build a consumer movement for non-fossil fuel-based electricity to power personal devices."

Senge suggested bringing two or three big device producers on board, and setting a goal to decarbonize the Internet in 20 years. "Hook up some of the biggest growth engines of electricity use to alternate energy, and then use them to pull the whole energy generation system." The key is getting the system moving. "It's a case of looking for places where massive change is already occurring, and then imagining how a large movement could really start to build." Even with massive changes, it will still take 50 to 100 years to slow and then gradually reverse the effects of climate change.

Senge referred to Australian environmentalist Paul Gilding's book, *The Great Disruption* and his TED talk entitled "The Earth is Full."[6] The former international president of Greenpeace has developed a crisis response strategy called The One Degree War Plan, which addresses the coming threat of global economic and geopolitical instability. Gilding believes climate change is a symptom of a growth mindset that has seen us expand our economies well beyond any material need. While there are many in the world with real material needs, they are not the ones driving this obscene growth.

Gilding has proposed reversing runaway climate change and starting to decarbonize by digging a new channel rather than trying to move a river. Forget environmental arguments—forget climate change, species destruction and ocean acidification—because we now know these environmental crises only lead to polarized political debate. Instead, let's focus on economics, mobilizing people by talking about their pocketbooks. Add up all the different costs that climate destabilization generates—not in the future but right now—the droughts, floods, settlers' camps that are needed because of droughts and flooding, all the strange storms, the hurricane-strength winds in Washington DC that cut power to six million people in the summer of 2013. Gilding suggested that if we would only get serious about actually adding up all these very diverse economic costs of climate destabilization, we might see that they are already crippling our economies. We don't have to wait 10 years to see this.

Applied systems thinking can be summarized in one word: leverage. In the example of climate change, Senge said we have a challenge to get the energy economy system moving in a different direction, quickly. People's need to argue is "usually driven by ego needs to be right and prove somebody else wrong." So, let's let go of these ego drives and stop trying to force feed people with opinions they cannot hold. Don't waste time talking to people who believe the world is so big and we are so small, we could not possibly alter global climate. "Go with people who are open-minded and are already predisposed to deep change…go to the young people."

He thinks young people will spearhead change and lead the energy revolution because they are the ones who will think it's crazy to have a car that gets less than 100 or 150 miles per gallon in the future, or will want fuel cell-powered motorcycles. Governments will follow with policy initiatives, and "it would have to be motivated or coordinated by a systems view so we don't waste time arguing."

Besides, who's future are we playing with anyway? he asked. We are gambling with young people's lives, which is why he suggests a strategy of bringing out the voices and encouraging the effective activism of people between 10 and 30. This will pay dividends because their voices resonate. The voices of young people have an emotional quality that moves us. "When young people say, 'You're gambling with my life' it brings adults up short. You can argue there is uncertainty, or the needed changes are going to cost a lot, or I'm just one person, what can I achieve? But it always comes down to the fact that it's their lives we are playing with."

The common denominator underlying a lot of these problems—whether the environmental crisis, or social justice, or the widening gap between rich and poor—is we don't seem able to develop wise, forward-thinking, strategies, he said. Our society systematically undervalues the future and is strongly biased towards short term. This is deeply connected to the fact that the voices of children and young people simply don't exist in our society. The future is not emotionally real to us. "The future is a bunch of statistics and projections—but that would change if children and young people got involved."

Encouraging youth involvement also dovetails with his strategy of focusing where the movement is happening. He talked about schools that are establishing systems-thinking programs, with sustainability as a foundation. The Kid's Footprint Project shows high school students how to map energy footprints, starting with their own school buildings, where they learn to analyze data and develop proposals for the return-on-investment of things like better lighting, better insulation, smart metering, and other basic nuts and bolts. "It's a learning laboratory, and the goal is to get them into their communities working with small and medium-sized businesses that can't afford significant energy rises."

Nine times out of ten when you have a conversation with a daughter or a granddaughter, a younger person, you see a pattern arise: What will the world be like for them? Adults start to look in the mirror, and one day they say, "Shit. What am I doing here?" It's really a personal question. If you are stuck in your role as the CEO, it's very hard to get creative or imagine a new perspective, Senge explained. "You can get so tied up in knots, trying to keep stakeholders and especially your shareholders happy. Your job depends upon your profit growth...."

Senge said when an adult has this kind of epiphany it's usually not because of any deep analysis. It's a realization, a kind of conviction in the heart that prompts them to suddenly say, "This is what I need to do." It becomes personal, matter-of-fact, and then they start thinking out of the box, looking at the larger system. "Unilever had a chairman who really got it personally. He was crystal clear. I remember him telling me, 'You know, I'm just trying to convince my people, if there's no fish, there's no fish sticks.'"

Change happens when something makes sense to you deeply, said Senge. So try to understand other people's logic, their reasoning, and gradually you will find a way to bring them along. "They may be keeping mum because their culture doesn't encourage it, or simply because they have not found what connects them to things they care about."

You can think in terms of the classic bell curve. "There are people who are engaged. At the other end of the curve, you have people who are really opposed. Then there are people who are predisposed but aren't yet engaged because they don't know how to be engaged. You don't have to convince them. You need to help them see how to connect. Then there could be a large number in the middle, people on the fence, who just don't understand what it's all about, how they can do something about it, and why it would make a difference from a practical standpoint." So, you target a few key folks in the later two groups and eventually find a way to reach them.

This is where you need skills in balancing advocacy and inquiry. For example, you would ask, How do you see this situation, and what are the questions that matter to you? Focus your communication on understanding where people are coming from and what truly matters to them. When appropriate ask their advice. "In short, create a real conversation, not a sales pitch. That's what an effective systems perspective looks like."

16

Listen Deeply

Otto SCHARMER *and* ANNE GIARDINI

"THE SUCCESS OF ANY intervention depends upon the interior condition of the intervener." This simple and perceptive statement summarizes what was an epiphany for Bill O'Brien, late CEO of Hanover Insurance and author of *Character at Work*.[1] O'Brien believed that the success of our actions does not depend so much on what we do, or how we do it, as it does on the inner place from which we operate.

Otto Scharmer often recounts this quote in the popular executive leadership workshops he facilitates around the world. The insight is central to Scharmer's work as a senior lecturer at MIT's Sloane School of Management. How can we access this inner source? What are the tools we need?

Scharmer's own first lesson in the connection of inner states with outer realities came when he was just 16 years old, and it has informed his work ever since. He grew up in northern Germany, where his parents were pioneers in organic biodynamic farming. One day while Scharmer was at school in Hamburg, the principal came to his class and said he should go home immediately. No one answered the phone at home when he called; nobody met him at the train; and for the first time in his life he took a taxi the final eight kilometers from the train station. Halfway home he could see the whole sky smudged with black, dark smoke rising from the place where his family's farm had been.

The young Scharmer leapt from the car and ran past hundreds of onlookers and firefighters. "I was unable to believe what my eyes actually told me was true...that the whole world I had been living in up to that point no longer existed. I still remember time slowing down and almost breaking a surface level of my mind and slowly sinking into my deeper mind." Scharmer realized that something enormous had ended, but he also understood that something else was beginning. "I realized how much my identity was attached to all these things that no longer existed," and in that same instant of awareness he suddenly recognized that the world that had vanished was not just outside him. He had lost something deep inside too, and with that realization came an intense experience of freedom. Scharmer was suddenly elevated, watching from above, and understood this loss went beyond the material dimension and had more to do with his essential self and the pure possibility of the future. "I had no idea that there was this other dimension that we can connect with under certain conditions."[2]

Scharmer has a PhD in economics and management, chairs the MIT Ideas program and is vice-chair of the World Economic Forum's Global Agenda Council on New Leadership. He founded the groundbreaking Presencing Institute, which coaches people in how to learn from the "emerging future," and has authored the best-selling book *Theory of U* and more recently *Leading from the Emerging Future: From Ego-System to Eco-System economies*.[3]

When Scharmer joined the MIT Learning Center founded by Peter Senge, he focused on what they call learning from the emerging future as opposed to the past, "and only then did I start to tap into my best work." Scharmer believes a connection to this deeper level of awareness—"a state with an entirely different texture and feeling"—is not only prompted by great loss but can also be spurred by social movements or a mission that makes people question why they are here, who they really are and what kind of journey they're on.

Reflecting on his early life, Scharmer recalled the nascent peace movement, green movement and fledgling anti-nuclear movement that were starting to emerge in Central Europe. How were these mobilized? Certainly not through facts, he determined. "That's the big myth." The quest for a new reality is achieved by connecting with the realm of possibilities, which involves inspiring new ways of operating, communicating and co-creating. A second myth is that a movement can be mobilized by filling people with fear, an approach the environmental movement has often employed in the past. Like so many others I talked with, Scharmer believes that trying to motivate people by frightening them—"It's even worse than you thought"—is no way to gain traction.

Scharmer believes we must open our minds, hearts and wills if we are to see our own blind spots, shift our awareness and connect with our best possible futures. And this is especially critical for leaders. Leadership training methodologies have long relied on historical lessons, but current challenges require new and different skills, an ability to let go of the past in order to connect and learn from *the emerging future*—the land of possibilities. With that in mind Scharmer developed the concept of *presencing*, a word he coined by blending the idea of "sensing," a feeling of the future possibilities, with presence, which is the state of being in the now. Together the two refer to sensing and actualizing one's highest future possibility, "acting from the presence of what is wanting to emerge." It's the idea of diving deeply and opening up, of transforming our thinking and gaining new insights into what is true entrepreneurial spirit.

Presencing means moving beyond our ingrained default positions and deep-rooted habits, judgments and thoughts. Old style of communication often leads to denial, cynicism or depression as people try to cope, Scharmer said. Yet some people manage to sense another reality and are able to connect with the energy of a different future. That is the essence of all creativity and entrepreneurship, he stressed: "You operate from a sense of possibilities, something that isn't there yet, and you put your own journey into the service of making it all happen, bringing it into reality. You remove everything that's getting in the way."

How do we sidestep denial, depression and fear of the future? How do we help people and communities move from one state to another, and carry that message into social systems and global initiatives? Scharmer believes a big part of the answer involves learning how to move beyond fear and loss. Such deep "systems change" is wrought through human relationships, projects, networks and pulling together.

All this sounds a bit esoteric, but Scharmer makes the experience real for business students by taking them on *empathy immersion* journeys, where they must confront extreme, raw, unfiltered situations. "In our world today there is no more cynical place than business schools that prepare people to go to Wall Street. As a matter of principle, I don't download any of my values on these people because that's just the next straitjacket. I create high-quality environments that allow students to investigate their own levels of knowing and connection with relevant pockets of society."

He takes them into edgy situations where they identify with people who are politically, ideologically and socially at the extreme opposite of everything the students hold sacred. There, they are urged to experience another person's life, to totally empathize, become one with others for a period of time. When they connect on more authentic levels with people who are radically different and have no aspirations about careers on Wall Street, the students cultivate new capacities and begin to operate from a deeper entrepreneurial impulse. Empathy immersion also helps people identify their true missions in life, rather than again downloading old models and operating on the basis of dusty frameworks.

Scharmer believes profound change and true leadership can evolve by moving through the deepening process he calls the *Theory U* which happens on three levels:

1. The level of the mind, which involves suspending old habits of judgment

**We go to the gym to train certain muscles,
and this is training the muscle of empathy,
getting out of old patterns.**

OTTO SCHARMER

2. Opening the heart and beginning to see problems through the eyes of other stakeholders, walking in others' shoes
3. Gaining the capacity to let go and let come

In the business realm, Scharmer explained that the latter is a key element. "The issue here is fear and holding on: fear of losing staff, of not making it, of failure, of being excluded from the community if you're not successful..." He has never seen this kind of fear in any start-up innovator, "because as an innovator you challenge the assumptions of your professional community."

Cambridge-educated lawyer and author Anne Giardini, who is Chancellor of Simon Fraser University in Vancouver, Canada and former president of Weyerhaeuser Company (one of the world's largest private owners of timberlands), is one of these switched-on leaders. She agrees we have to change the way we see the world and how we perceive others, and believes in deflecting people from adversarial techniques and guiding them toward constructive, trustful dialogue and a meeting of minds. Giardini finds the current acrimony and polarization around environment issues "enormously dismaying, immature and distressing."[4]

Whether you're governing a country, a province, a city or a company you should govern for everyone, not just one part of it, she said. And that means finding common ground. Maybe you've got to devise a new common ground or something that you genuinely believe could be common. "I think one of the best things about leadership and the best opportunities you have as a leader is to take problems out of the trenches and up two to three levels. I think people should all be sent to school to relearn that, in order to look at things from a much more mature, higher level, and from a longer-term point of view."

Scharmer explained that the English root for the word leadership means, "to go forth, to cross the threshold." But he also traced the word through its Indo-European roots in a different translation and found it literally also means "to die." Essentially leadership is the ultimate process of letting go and letting come. "It's letting go of one world that we know very well and stepping into the territory of the unknown. This is the quality that experienced entrepreneurial leaders have, and it's the collective first-person experience we have as a global community today vis-à-vis challenges in climate change.... That is the capacity to deal with issues around which there is fear."

The three-part process of Theory U can broaden and deepen our view of a situation. Next, we should seek to connect all that we observe and experience together with deep reflection, contemplative practices that move people into intentional stillness. "Basically you give everyone, as an individual and as a community, quality time to focus on what matters most…What is it that, for me, and my own journey is most essential? Basically it is letting go of all the noise that is nothing."

Scharmer believes the environmental movement has missed out on this deeper awareness dimension and advises creating "high-quality reflection spaces for groups and individuals, with different stakeholders going on that journey together, where there really is a possibility for the system to see itself." Scharmer's definition of dialogue is not two or three people talking to each other. It is the capacity of people to reflect on and to see themselves as part of a larger ecosystem, to recognize how their own behaviors and assumptions shape what's going on. "It's like switching on an awareness outside of myself."

Scharmer told me that moving through the Theory U process can lead to elegant results. A system that was previously bogged down by people working from ego, seeking to optimize their own careers or blindly following institutional interests or agendas, can begin to change. Individuals can start the process of co-creation as they move from ego-system awareness to ecosystem awareness.

How exactly does this wisdom help us deal with the change resistance problems we face in the world today?

When people connect intensely with others who are different from them, they begin to operate from a more profound entrepreneurial impulse. "You begin to experience yourself in a deeper way, to sense a possibility in yourself that you weren't aware of before. That deeper level of awareness is already there. We just need to remove the rubble, all the noise that keeps us from attending to that." He said that the process builds confidence and greater creativity, better problem solving ideas.

How do we open our minds and hearts so we can connect on deeper levels?

"It's an improvisation," Scharmer responded, but on a practical level it starts with genuine conversation and relationship building. Fifty percent of his classwork is about listening, helping people move from judgmental listening, where you just pay attention to what you already know, to factual listening, which is when you begin to see something new. This leads to empathetic listening where people begin to see a situation in the eyes of another, and finally to what he calls generative listening. This is listening in a way that allows something new to happen, something that hasn't quite manifested yet. The process requires people to open their minds and suspend rigid and narrow former habits; to open their hearts and begin to see through the lens of other stakeholders, to walk in other's shoes, particularly those of the most marginalized; and thirdly, to "open the will," to let go and let come.

Listening becomes "effective" and is actually a kind of birthing process because it leads to something that did not exist before, Scharmer explained. In this sense it is co-creative. Generative listening can give voice to what is about to happen, what is about to emerge. It is a kind of event in the making.

Scharmer believes listening is foundational, not only for leadership, but for mastery in any kind of profession. In all creative projects and applications it is the most important and relevant of skills. You will know you have achieved something if you leave a conversation with far more energy than you entered it. After truly generative interaction with another person, you are no longer the same. You're closer to who you really are. "There is a subtle letting go of the 'old me' and a keener connection to Self (with a capital 'S') which is my highest future possibility." When we lose track of who we are we become exhausted, burned out, depressed. Reconnection to the authentic self switches on high energy. "So you practice, practice, practice. It may sound a bit abstract, and it's not something you can perfect in ten minutes," he warned, but mastering generative dialogue is as satisfying as learning to play a musical instrument.

Scharmer said this kind of listening skill is important whenever there is a culture clash or divide where social or economic systems are breaking down. He emphasized that generative listening is definitely not focused on fixing anything or problem solving: "That's the big inhibitor of change, and another big myth." He called the urge to fix "the problem of problem solving." Empathetic listening does not mean offering palliative statements such as: "Hey, I know exactly what you're talking about and here's what you need to do." Instead, Scharmer suggested that the goal is to mobilize energy around creating something successful, perhaps in a community context or as a collective function. "It's a more subtle dimension of leadership, and one which has been largely ignored in the past."

Listening in such dialogue would be useful in the environmental movement where much of the talk in past years has centered on sustainability, doing things less badly. A more inspiring and successful viewpoint would be to envision a future that is worth committing to, that features a series of reframed economic activities around what matters in life, such as happiness and well-being. Such a focus would encourage the dimension of mindfulness in a very natural way, Scharmer said.

He advised that the environmental movement should not be about forcing something down the throat of anyone, which leads invariably to resistance and people getting stuck in their own positions. It should focus instead on people who are ready to participate, willing to take action. "Go where the change is already taking place," he said, echoing the words of Peter Senge.

Scharmer's goal is to help people find and identify conditions that allow small, incremental changes. Institutions need to look for the cracks too, gateways or openings that are made critical and timely because old behaviors and routines no longer create results. Institutions can become willing to put their attention here, and commit resources to trying out new ways of operating and collaborating.

The way to leverage change is to shift the inner place from which we operate. When we deepen our own listening, we engage in a conversation that affects people differently. We shift the quality of awareness and attention away from resistance interaction and resistance intervention. This new field is where the greatest potential impact for change lies, and where we need to place our attention. It's the blind spot in all leadership. "This is where—through small experiments—we have found a whole bunch of very usable methods and tools that we can make accessible to people."

In a paper prepared for the 2010 World Economic Forum, Scharmer talked about this blind spot in institutional leadership.[5] He said today's leaders and change makers are caught between two worlds: they are confronting unprecedented 21st-Century challenges, with inadequate 20th-Century management tools. They are struggling to bridge the gap, but he said the biggest problem is a lack of collective leadership "to draw together all key stakeholders and involve them in a process that begins with uncovering common intention and ends with collectively creating profound innovation."

Scharmer called this missing capacity the scarcest resource in society today. It is a quality that is not being nurtured, and little focus is given to its development anywhere in our system of higher education. Business schools focus on leadership, public policy and the social sector, but nowhere do all these intersect. We need all three if we are to address and solve the pressing challenges of our time, and without them we will continue to produce results that nobody wants: poverty, pollution and institutional paralysis.

The Mighty Tool
of Public Narrative

17

The Myth of Apathy

with RENEE LERTZMAN

BEING GREEN IS attractive, desirable and profitable, said environmental communications specialist Renee Lertzman. But it is also potentially frightening because it threatens what many of us hold dear, what is central to how we construct meaning in our lives. So being green creates anxiety. Lertzman has studied the deep, psychological dimensions of sustainability, and we discussed why people fail to take action on severe environmental threats, why no nation has managed to adequately reduce carbon emissions and why instead we see international and national indifference and lack of knowledge.

Change resistance is complicated, explained Lertzman, who has a master's in communication studies from the University of North Carolina and a doctorate in social sciences from Cardiff University in Wales. She said the current shortage of engagement, activation or inspiration is typically framed in terms that reflect a lack of something, the idea that people don't care enough about what's happening. She disagrees with this diagnosis, and has blamed the situation on what she calls the *Myth of Apathy*. It's a concept that arose during her doctoral research, which took her to a "very degraded" and industrial part of Wisconsin. Her study was conducted in the Great Lakes region, where she recorded a high level of frustration among activists who felt people were not sufficiently mobilized or engaged when

What if we presume that people do care, very deeply, and about many of the same things we care about?

RENEE LERTZMAN

addressing serious threats to the lakes. She surveyed thousands of people in Green Bay and followed up with in-depth interviews with those who knew something about what was going on but were not particularly engaged. Her work has been featured in *The New York Times*, Dot Earth, KBOO Radio, and *The Ecologist*, and she has been a visiting fellow at the Portland Center for Public Humanities. Lertzman also serves on the editorial board of *Ecopsychology*.[1]

Renee Lertzman did not set out to explore the values, belief systems or opinions of Wisconsin residents but rather their actual experience about where they lived, their water, their air quality. Her study, however, led to revelations about all kinds of "complex, contradictory, messy experiences, feelings and perceptions" that suddenly made it obvious there was no clear apathy. What she discovered instead was a huge amount of concern about what was going on with the Great Lakes, with the water, with the environment, and a perplexing mood of loss—a sense of mourning, melancholy and nostalgia. Lertzman found a lot of tension too. People loved the lakes, wanted to fish there and wanted them to be clean, but they were caught in a dilemma because many a family member worked in the paper mill that was destroying the water quality. The mill gave them their livelihood.

And so a premise about the Myth of Apathy began to take shape. Lertzman has come to believe that apathy is constructed and perceived as an "enemy" or dragon that must be slain. "It's like we have to fight our way through this pervasive apathy in order to get people to care," and yet her research found the opposite. She now poses the question: "What if we presume that people do care, very deeply, and about many of the same things we care about?"[2] This new train of thought explains why current narratives fail: They are based on a misguided perception that apathy is a serious hurdle.

Lertzman urged us all to ask, What if the lack of involvement in climate change has come about because this care and concern is not expressed or acknowledged? If we presume there is a surplus of care and concern and a desire to make things right, how does that change the way environmental advocates conduct our communication strategy? "It becomes more about how can we support, invite, cultivate and channel rather than this impossible task of getting people to care."

Lertzman suggested that branding people as apathetic is not only erroneous but also disrespectful and patronizing. It's a lazy approach because such an assessment is rooted in our tendency to make snap judgments; it also assumes that people do and say what they actually want. "I know this might sound strange, but that's just not the case." Why we do what we do is complicated, so really, the Myth of Apathy is about reframing the question of care. What would happen if we started to act on the assumption that there is a surplus of concern, an overabundance of energy to be tapped into and an earnest desire to make things right—not a lack? Lertzman believes this different point of view could create a tectonic shift in our communications strategy.

Of course, there is such a thing as apathy, and Lertzman mentioned the work of American psychiatrist Harold Searles, one of the first clinicians to talk about how the ecological crisis deeply affects people. Influential papers that he wrote in 1972 describe how some humans are hampered by a sense of apathy, but Searles saw that as a symptom, a defense mechanism just like projection. "If we recognize apathy as a symptom, this is another piece of the picture," said Lertzman, who added there is much to learn about people's conflicts and tensions.[3] "It is easy to blame others and say something is all their fault," but in the case of climate denial, she said, there is real hatred circulating and being projected onto others, and this can lead to apathy in some people.

Lertzman suggested that these insights help expand our thinking and spirit of enquiry. What would our world look like if we were curious about what people actually deeply feel? Most of us don't even know what's going on in our own minds, let alone others' minds, and are completely unaware of our unconscious wellsprings of inner conflicts and tensions. Are people feeling sad, or anxious, or angry—and how do we determine that?

We can begin by drawing out people's stories and narratives, Lertzman said, using this new understanding to change the tone and language of our approach. We can do this on a societal level, too, by translating our tone into something more invitational, truth-eliciting and acknowledging. Lertzman is not opposed to incentives like taxes and other external prods, but she believes they are superficial compared to this kind of deeper work. "I'm talking about going to a more fundamental level of what constitutes behavior in the first place, which is how we construct and produce meaning in our lives."

For instance, how do we encourage people in a building to use less electricity and less water and recycle more? Of course we can try to tweak behavior through external stimuli or prods, but we are more effective when we bring deep meaning into the process. This approach would look at the narrative of a building, its story and history, what it feels like to live there and be part of that community. "This is tapping into meaning, and it can become something that really makes sense because I am part of the building. I am wearing this relationship."

Real and lasting change is not imposed. It emerges, said Renee Lertzman. "And it's not about lack, it's about what we create. It's a very positive, generative narrative that taps into our innate desire to be part of something bigger than us." We don't generate meaning on our own, or in a vacuum. We create it together, in relationships, in interactions. Meaning is co-constructed and produces a sense of connection, cohesion and validation because we feel part of something larger. We connect with people better when we communicate at a deeper level, when we are meaning centered.

I asked Renee Lertzman if outing climate change deniers is a good tactic, and she advised it has its place, when done with compassion. "Compassion is the only way to adequately and effectively engage with ignorance—because that's what we're talking about here, in a spiritual sense, not a literal one. This is ignorance of who we are and the reality of our connection to everything." That kind of ignorance can lead to tremendous destruction. There's something very violent about climate denial and it almost certainly arises from fear and anxiety, Lertzman suggested. As Bryant Welch noted in his book, *State of Confusion*, hatred can be a defense against feeling confused.

This is very sensitive territory, Lertzman warned. If you push on a defense such as this, it will push back. We always resist change, even positive change that brings growth and development, because we try to valiantly protect what we think needs protecting or we feel is at stake. Yet criticizing climate change deniers is a crucial function, just as it was when people spoke the truth about the Holocaust. Lertzman referred to eminent British psychoanalyst Hanna Segal who said silence is the real crime.[4] But Lertzman suggested that we should speak in a way that is compassionate, while not letting people off the hook. As the Dalai Lama says, "compassion can be very fierce." We need to practice compassion for ourselves too, and be concerned about our own anger or impatience, she said.

Compassion helps us understand what's really causing the inaction—the fact that we're caught up in a series of complicated dilemmas and tensions, contradictory drives and anxieties that we are unable to sort out or negotiate. "We need to begin to recognize what's being asked of us in terms of how we manage and negotiate these tensions, which are very deep in our identity and part of who we are as human beings."

Such inner drives are not rational and they go far beyond surface emotions, to a less conscious level. "We are dealing with any number of ecological threats that are deeply anxiety producing. It seems totally obvious to say that, but it's as if this piece has been completely overlooked." We consistently focus on tuning into people's rationality or their knowledge, or we try and appeal to their self-interest, to basically manipulate and engage behavior. We're not actually appreciating with compassion what we're really talking about. "We're skipping over that experience of fear."

Lertzman explained that psychoanalysis's concept of *splitting* is useful when thinking about sustainability. Splitting describes how we tend to split off anxiety, emotional loss, feelings that are scary. For example, some environmentalists tend to see things in terms of black and white, good versus evil, "so they can sidestep dealing with the really messy reality of sorting through difficult change."

Lertzman reiterated that all change can provoke anxiety, even if it's positive or productive, like moving into a nicer house or taking a better job. All change involves anxiety and loss, as well as gains in opportunity or growth. And the shifts involving climate change are ultimately much more worrying because they require some recognition that humanity has done wrong. For some, there could be an intolerable sense of guilt, "the fact we've really effed up."

And so Lertzman suggested that the issue of climate change is both psychological and social. This change is immensely anxiety producing—"It is almost in a class of its own" because we're talking about change in response to human-generated circumstances that we know are life-destroying. Asking people to confront that and deal with it is asking them to take some responsibility for what's happened. "I don't think we see much capacity for that socially, culturally, individually," because people find it too overwhelming. So, there is guilt and impotence, combined with a lack of political will and inaction among government and business leaders. "It's a protective strategy to distance oneself from that which causes this sense of powerlessness."

Self-protection can manifest in denial, projection and splitting, Lertzman said, which are all defensive mechanisms and strategies. Sociologist Kari Norgaard described these strategies as not being just our own, individual psychology, but aspects that are performed socially, organizationally and politically. In other words, we need each other to collude in our denial, to help manage our anxiety, said Lertzman. Norgaard also said silence on the subject of climate change should not be interpreted as disinterest, but rather as something people find too painful to acknowledge because of their role in causing it.[5]

I asked what happens if people can't avoid these feelings. How can people, groups and organizations feel safe enough to tolerate and face up to tough environmental issues? She said this is where clinical psychology and new clinically inspired research offers insights and "potent tenets," many of which she has written about in *The Ecologist*.[6]

What does a therapist do when working one on one with a client who brings harmful, self-protective attitudes into a session? They do three things, Lertzman explained:

1. acknowledge
2. encourage the truth
3. support and mobilize

Acknowledgment involves saying, "I hear you, I see you and I reflect back to you what I think you're feeling." That simple act is powerful in helping disarm defense mechanisms. When we feel heard and supported we soften a bit; we become a little more receptive, have a little more access to what our own experience is, rather than feeling we have to defend. Related to acknowledgment is the second tenet, which is the need to uncover the truth. The therapist supports a person as they speak the truth, and provides a sense of "working through this together." And finally a therapist demonstrates leadership and strength, and as an example Lertzman recalled Winston Churchill's famous "We shall fight on the beaches" speech. Here Churchill talked about a military disaster and warned of possible invasion by the Germans, yet spoke magnificently about defending "our island home and riding out the storm of war." Lertzman said the statesman did not cover up recent losses and defeats or deny the reality of the situation, but painted a picture of heroism and strength in moving forward.

So this technique involves revealing the truth, no matter how dire, acknowledging it and tapping into proactive solutions. She said it's important to focus on possibilities, on what can be done. "It's like being the rah-rah cheerleader. There has to be some element of truth telling, an acknowledgment of the reality of the situation and that other piece of moving forward. One without the other is incomplete and limited. We point out innovations, possibilities, potentials and say, Let's move forward. Let's be champions."

18

Psychic Numbing

with PAUL SLOVIC

P AUL SLOVIC is an expert in human judgment and decision-
making. He is president of Decision Research, has been president of the Society for Risk Analysis and is a professor of psychology
at University of Oregon.[1] Slovic's research looks at how the general public and experts perceive perils and threats very differently,
and offers critical lessons for those involved in risk perception and
communication, including insights into why we fail to respond to
large-scale international tragedies. His most recent work looks at
what he calls *psychic numbing*; according to Slovic, psychic numbing
helps explain why we fail to respond to mass atrocities and crises
like climate change.

I asked Slovic, Why are we glued to our television sets, cells and
tablets when a small child is trapped in a well for 58 hours, yet yawn
and switch channels when more than 500,000 are slaughtered in
Rwanda over the course of 100 days? What is the role of emotions
and cognition when it comes to our conceptions of danger and problems that are enormous in scope, and how has his work concerning
biotechnology, prescription drugs, terrorism, nanotechnology and
more guided his own thinking?

Slovic said there are many large-scale, worldwide problems that
affect us both close to home and abroad, and that we tune out. There
is no single reason why. "We're talking about an underreaction to

problems that are large in scope,"[2] and this is starkly different from what happens at a community level, where we typically have a strong and immediate reaction to violence, after a murder for instance. "We've got a system of law enforcement that tracks down perpetrators and brings them to justice. We've got laws and institutions that are very strong and aggressive at the local level. But we have little or nothing like that at the international level." Slovic believes this has contributed to a string of genocides dating back to 1915.

Slovic argues the "psychic numbing" phenomenon, the difficulty we have with emotionally connecting to problems that are large in scale, is highly relevant to species extinction too. Do we really have to wait until we are looking at the world's last polar bear standing on a small piece of ice, before we'll take seriously the extinction possibility for these animals? Why don't we act when the problem is still in the thousands? Again, it relates to his premise that we react strongly to individuals in distress, but don't take action when problems exist for thousands.

There is no simple reason for this indifference, although Slovic believes that numbers alone, "dry statistics," do little to communicate the true meaning of atrocities. They don't spark emotion or feeling and thus fail to motivate action.

We need strong guidelines and laws, Slovic suggested, because it's not a question of not wanting to do the right thing or not valuing people. We value people very highly in some cases, "but despite the high value we place on individuals, we don't seem able to act, to ramp that up in scale." When numbers soar, our consistency with basic values and concerns collapses. Most people are caring and highly responsive when they hear of an individual's desperate plight, yet are numbly indifferent when one person becomes many. Slovic explained that this was evident in the Darfur region of western Sudan, when more than 200,000 people were murdered by government-sponsored militias.[3]

One of the obvious barriers to involvement and decisive action is what Slovic refers to as the drop-in-the-bucket effect. "The problem is so big, and I'm so small. It won't make much difference, no matter what I do." He sees this response every day in the work he does around global violence and believes this attitude may affect response to climate change and other large-scale environmental problems.

It may even be easy for those of us in the West to be numbed relating to climate change and other global environmental problems because we are not feeling physical effects in any immediate or distinct way. It's easier to see soaring temperatures as extremes of natural variation, rather than significant developments worldwide. "There's a great temptation to view it [any incident] in a way that's most comfortable for us, so we say nothing's really changed." That way we don't have to sacrifice anything that we like doing. A lot of people feel their interests will be threatened if we get tough on pollution, restrict activities or change technologies out of concern for the planet's environment. "Powerful people would be hurt economically, their industries would be hurt. So, it's a battle."

Slovic co-authored a paper with Columbia University's Elke Weber regarding risk perception, and I asked him to describe the difference between how an expert evaluates risk and how a layperson perceives it.[4] "On issues like cigarette smoking, the public and the experts were pretty much on the same page, but issues involving radiation, chemicals and biotech revealed strong differences." He found that whether people are exposed voluntarily or not to a hazard will affect their attitudes, as will the potential outcome and whether it is catastrophic or just affects a few individuals.

"A lot of specific qualities of a hazard are important to the public and less important to the experts." For instance, experts tend to concentrate on probabilities that something will go wrong, the size of consequences, mortality, morbidity and anticipated losses. They are very calculating in their approach and focus on a small number of factors. But riskiness means a lot more to people than mere statistics. The public is sensitive to issues such as personal control. They want to know if they are deriving any benefit from an activity that puts them at risk. They want to know if they bear the risk while someone else is getting the benefit. Qualitative factors of personal benefit and fairness influence public perception and acceptance of risk too.

When Slovic and Weber looked at qualities of hazards that influence perception and acceptance, one thing that stood out was the element of dread, which Slovic found is one of the best predictors of the perception and acceptance of risk. Over time, he came to appreciate more and more how important this was. He began studying perception of risk in the late 1970s, and by the 1990s was focusing not only on dread, but also on broader concepts that resulted in his book, *The Feeling of Risk*.[5] Here Slovic explored the interaction of emotion and cognition relative to risk perception. He found that elements of knowledge, cognitive skill and communication are necessary when making good decisions in the face of risk—but he underscored it is almost impossible to understand risk without taking emotional components into account.

The statistics in climate change discussion, besides being confusing, lack emotion. Few people grasp the impact of global atmospheric concentrations of carbon dioxide passing 400 parts per million—but tell them about greater glacier melt, rising sea levels, more droughts and hurricanes, more mosquitos spreading malaria and dengue fever, and the true meaning of the crisis hits home. Emotion can motivate people to take action, and hopefully prevent even greater disasters.

"What has become clear over years of work is the importance of emotion and feeling—this is where risk resides in us most of the time," said Slovic. We rarely do mental calculations of risk. We rely instead on a gut feeling whether it's safe to overtake a car on the highway, or eat that food that has been in the refrigerator too long. We use our senses and our feelings, and that skill stretches far back in the evolution of the human species. It's how evolving humans judged risk for millions of years. "Our brain evolved a way of processing information via feelings that is quite sophisticated and effective in many cases. But over time, we also evolved the capability of thinking about and dealing with risk in a more analytical way." We developed probability theory, mathematics, symbolic reasoning. And that led

There is the drop-in-the-bucket effect:
The problem is so big, and I'm so small.
It won't make much difference, no matter what I do.
So, why don't I just do whatever is comfortable.

PAUL SLOVIC

to risk assessment as an analytic domain, and then toxicology, epidemiology, environmental science. So our brain now operates using both of these remarkable qualities; scientific knowledge and method function alongside structures that allow us to make judgments based on feeling. Analysis and calculation can take us to the Moon or Mars. That's not done with feeling. That's science, Slovic said.

Most of the time we judge risk in our personal lives with our gut—but science is vital too, Slovic stressed. He illustrated his point by explaining that human vision is a very sophisticated capability, and most of the time it is very accurate and rational. However, in some situations there are visual patterns that deceive the eye. "You look at something and you think that A is bigger than B, when in fact B is bigger than A because of the context; the visual system can be misled.... Our emotional system, for reacting to people in need—which is primarily tuned to protecting people around us—breaks down in the context of distant, large-scale, anonymous suffering. Just like a visual illusion, it's kind of a moral illusion." We can hear about things, watch the news broadcast and then turn our backs and deal with our concerns. We forget about the bigger picture, especially if there's nothing immediate we can do. It's like a moral illusion that everything is okay, when in fact it's not.

When it comes to climate change Slovic sees a future that is so problematic we should start taking action now. He believes problems of global warming, species extinction and pollution require slow, deliberate, analytical thinking, not fast gut reactions, which tend to be so much easier for us and are typically delivered with great confidence. Slovic recommended Daniel Kahneman's best-seller, *Thinking, Fast and Slow*,[6] which described how we process information: quickly and intuitively, versus slowly and thoughtfully. Kahneman's research demonstrated the differences between these methods and some of the problems inherent in fast thinking. Slovic and Kahneman edited a book with Amos Tversky called *Judgment under Uncertainty: Heuristics and Biases*.[7]

To the extent that people will continue to rely on feelings emanating from fast thinking, Slovic believes we need to make climate data more emotionally gripping. Cold facts and statistics need to be wrapped in individual stories, personal accounts, emotional images that have the power to "penetrate and impact the fast system." He's not suggesting that people ignore the numbers, "but don't make them salient." You have to make them personal to convey feeling. When you see a number, it has to have a tinge of emotion behind it that tells you this number is either "something very good or something very bad." If a number doesn't carry feeling, we don't really understand it, and we won't act on it.

The element of strong emotion is also what makes humans experience dread, said Slovic. We spend a lot more money to study and prevent cancer than we do to prevent certain types of accidents, which are just as deadly and horrific, because cancer has more "dread quality." While studying terrorism, he found that an anthrax attack is more "dreadful" for people than a bomb because anthrax is invisible, and its scope is unknown, whereas a bomb is more contained. "Some things are more dreaded than others because they carry stronger feelings, relating to how much work we have to do to prevent them."

So Slovic urged sensitive communicators to present information in a way that touches emotions and makes things imaginable—for example, the dreadfulness of a world that is dangerously polluted. "We see things happening now with drought in the US. But again, a drought is something that many of us still feel pretty distant from, although certainly not the people who are experiencing it. There are two ways to go: One is to focus on sensitizing fast-thinking people, also called System One thinkers. We can speak to them through vivid images, emotion, stories and narratives. The other is to approach the problem with System Two thinkers, the scientific deliberators, where we step back and say, 'Let's think more carefully about this problem, and bring science into the picture and analysis.'"

Clearly we need both fast and slow thinking, emotional and analytical skills, to address major problems, but it is important to understand that fast thinking lulls us into complacency. If we take the time to sit down and do some careful, slow thinking we could expand laws and institutions that would aggressively pursue problems, and we wouldn't have to always be emotionally reactive. If you have created a system of laws and institutions based on thoughtful evaluation of what your values are for certain outcomes, then they take over and run day and night, regardless of how you're feeling.

"I argue in the violence area that we don't have such effective laws and institutions at the international level," he said. "We thought we had it in the United Nations as an institution, and it's basically impotent. We thought we had it in the Genocide Convention as a rule of law, and that's been found to be impotent. So we're leaving it to our feelings, and basically our feelings are worrying more about the Olympics or whatever than about what's going on in Syria."

Slovic suggested that we need laws and institutions in the environmental arena for the same reason. We need people around the table who think slowly and deliberately about where we're headed in this world, what kind of future we're creating for our descendants and what kind of laws and institutions we need to make this future less ominous, rather than depending on fickle feelings of the moment, which are very distracting.

"We need the analytic structure of laws and institutions," he said flatly, offering another analogy: We know taxes are important for the functioning of government so we don't leave it to individual feelings. We have a very quantitative, calculated, analytic system that tells each of us, based on our income, what we are obligated to pay. And then, it's backed up by the force of law—not that there aren't loopholes—but that's the idea. You don't leave it to feelings. It's done through analysis and supported by legal institutions.

I noted that in *Climate Cover-Up* and DeSmogBlog we tell stories that aren't just about big environmental problems. They are about gaming the system, about being manipulated and hoodwinked. I asked if this is an easier issue to get people concerned about than climate change.

"Yes, because what you're doing is providing information that, if people are paying attention, should make then angry, and anger is a powerful emotion." Those manipulating information are putting their self-interest ahead of you and your family, your children, your grandchildren. Something that makes people angry is a motivator for action, for fighting back in some way. So that's important. "We see this in the tobacco area, where I think one of the factors that tipped the balance in the last 20-something years was the finding that secondhand smoke is harmful, so it's no longer just the smokers harming themselves, but they are exporting the risk to non-smokers, which is unfair. You get this element of unfairness, which is again part of the risk related to acceptable risk."

After a long career studying human nature and risk, is Slovic hopeful that we can deal with these issues eventually? What he is finding and documenting is a complexity of issues involving risk, uncertainty and high stakes. If we don't understand that complexity and how it works we are going to be buffeted by things we can't control. "That is very worrisome. But as we understand more, we gain the ability to potentially manage this important domain of risk and complexity. It doesn't guarantee that we're going to do it, but through greater understanding we have a better chance of shaping the future in a better way."

19

Sometimes David Wins

with MARSHALL GANZ

LONG AGO, on the steep shores of an ancient valley called Elah, in what is now Israel, the Philistine army was assembled and preparing to do battle. Their greatest warrior, a nine-foot giant called Goliath, was hurling insults at the Israelites, taunting them to come out and fight, but his opponents were cowering in terror, frozen with dread. Young David, a shepherd who had come to bring lunch to his warrior brothers, was outraged by the abuse and decided to act. He volunteered to fight the giant, and although King Saul had some doubts, he agreed to let the youth fight if he used the king's own armor. David dutifully put on the king's helmet and breastplate, picked up his shield and heavy sword but found he couldn't move. That's when he noticed five smooth stones at his feet. He remembered who he was, a shepherd not a soldier, who had learned to defend his flock against wolf and bear with stones and a sling. He took off the armor, picked up the stones, and turned to face Goliath. In his arrogance, Goliath began to laugh—"You send a boy with a stick to face me"—but his laughter was cut short by a stone in the forehead. David then grasped the giant's own sword and sliced off his head.

This is a favorite story of renowned social justice advocate Marshall Ganz, the brilliant community organizer whose framework was the basis of President Obama's winning ground game campaigns of 2007–8 and who has contributed to many other movements in the United States and around the world. Why does Ganz choose this particular story when teaching a class on leadership, organizing and action at Harvard's Kennedy School of Government? Because it shows how resourcefulness—fueled by courage, commitment and imagination—can overcome nominally powerful resources, as well as the arrogance that often goes with them.

"The fact is, David sometimes wins,"[1] said Ganz, adding that the young hero of this tale did not have a plan all figured out at the beginning, but he emerged victorious because he found his authentic self and shed the borrowed weaponry. David was skilled in the use of a slingshot, and because he was a shepherd, not a soldier, he saw the battlefield through different eyes. He knew what he was doing, was prepared for it, strategically creative in his use of power and found resources in a few stones: "David's heart enabled him to devise a strategy that worked, and he had the skilled hands to carry it out. Without the strategy the story wouldn't be enough."

Ganz believes it is through narratives such as this one that people learn to access the moral and emotional resources we need to act with agency in the face of danger, challenge and threat. Those resources can be found in our own lived experience, in how we have dealt with our own pain and where we have found hope. Such narratives describe how we become inspired leaders in the face of uncertainty. They are gateways through which we learn about courage and hope, about what we stand for, who we really are and why we should take action. "They are the portals on the transcendent."

Ganz's theory of public narrative is one of the most important lessons set out in *I'm Right*, and is a mighty tool for leadership and change. An urgent need to improve narrative skills is painfully clear after looking at all the barriers to communication and action I have described. Weak storytelling skills and mistaken ideas about the power of facts not only leave the public unmoved, but they can also trigger antagonism and contribute to polarization and ineffective advocacy. Strong narrative skills can, however, not only deliver an inspiring message for change but also counteract PR and disinformation. We have a better chance of sidestepping the advocacy trap and avoiding the triggering of psychological barriers if we stay strongly rooted in the values that emerge from our own story.

I sought out Ganz to ask how we can better connect with people in difficult conversations. His initial response was not what I expected. It was rooted in his own story and his exposure to many inspiring messages at a young age. Born in 1943 in Bay City Michigan, Ganz lived with his family in Germany for three years after the Second World War. His father was a rabbi and an army chaplain who worked with Holocaust survivors, "and as a child I met people whose lives had been destroyed, who were looking for some way to find enough hope to restore them." One of his first memories was of his fifth birthday in a camp for people who had been displaced, amid many other youngsters. Ganz did not realize until much later why there were no parents present.

After graduating from high school in Bakersfield, California, where his family moved when he was eight, Ganz won a scholarship to Harvard in 1960, the same year John Kennedy was elected President of the US. Ganz was captivated by the President's rousing message about a new generation of leadership. Stirred by the 1963 March on Washington, the Battle of Birmingham, the murder of civil rights leader Medgar Evers and, finally, the assassination of the young Kennedy, Ganz was drawn into the Civil Rights Movement, in part because his parents had interpreted the Holocaust to him not simply as a form of anti-Semitism but from the broader perspective that racism kills. "It's not a very complex idea, but it's a very true one—and the Civil Rights Movement was, of course, challenging institutionalized racism in this country," said Ganz. "So that was a no-brainer."

As a youth Ganz grew up hearing the story of Exodus told every Passover, and came to understand that this journey from slavery to freedom was not simply an account of one time, one place or one people, but a story that has been retold and reenacted from generation to generation. The US Civil Rights Movement spoke to the nation in the language of Exodus.

Marshall Ganz volunteered for the 1964 Mississippi Summer Project, leaving university a year before graduation. He began working in civil rights, where he learned the difference between charity and justice, that power without love is never just and that, likewise, any love that doesn't take power seriously can never achieve justice. He became part of a movement in which power mattered, and he realized nothing would change unless something was done about the basic political, economic and cultural powerlessness of the black community.

Through the Bus Boycott, a social protest campaign led by Martin Luther King, who was just 25 at the time, Ganz gleaned a fundamental insight into collective power. Ganz realized that if people used their feet to get on a bus they empowered a bus company, whereas if they used their feet to stay off the bus and walk to work, they empowered themselves. "Things begin to change when people find a way to use their resources to shift, to turn their dependency into interdependence." This is a craft that can bring communities together and empower people to begin solving their own problems.

In 1991 Ganz went back to university, finished his senior year in history and government, wrote his thesis and graduated at age 49. Now bitten by the education bug, he followed up with a master's at Kennedy School, then a PhD in sociology at Harvard, where he ended up joining the faculty. He has been teaching ever since, first developing courses on leadership, organizing and action and more recently on the unique role of narrative.

Immersed in the study of what motivates people, in what are the primary drivers of social movements, and having been steeped in the Exodus story, Ganz put together a class on public narrative and hoped a few students would register. When 35 showed up for the first class, he realized he had touched a nerve. "I was onto something, and then the Obama campaign came along—and it was a great way to figure out how you get lots of people to understand how to use

**If you are in public life
you must learn to tell your own story.
If you don't, others will, and you'll turn
over authorship of your story to others
whose interests may differ from your own.**

MARSHALL GANZ

narrative." In the fall of 2015, 130 students, from 31 different countries, enrolled in this course.

Narrative is a form of empowering discourse through which we learn to exercise agency itself. It is a mindful response to a challenge, as opposed to a fearful one. A public story can help create collective agency by linking together the speaker's story of self, the community's story of us and the challenge's story of now. Such public narrative starts with a story of self because, Ganz stressed, "If you are in public life you must learn to tell your own story. If you don't, others will, and you'll turn over authorship of your story to others whose interests may differ from your own." As illustrated by his own story in this chapter, a *story of self* communicates the values that call an individual to action. It should speak to the heart and describe our unique experience: the challenges we have faced, the choices we've made and the outcomes that unfolded during our journey though life. This story of self explains not only why we are called to our work but also how we see ourselves connecting to it, which in turn enables others to connect with it through us.

Next, in the *story of us*, a group can animate the values shared by our constituency. Through stories of joint experience, that everyone recognizes, this narrative creates a sense of the values we share, that are common to our community. It explains how we are connected to each other. As in the story of self, the idea is to tell a specific tale of challenge, of choice, and outcome, with rich details of specific people, time and place that bring attention to common values.

And finally, a *story of now* turns the present moment into a narrative moment where "we are confronted by a challenge and must find sources of hope and the courage to act." The challenge creates anxiety, tension and the question is, Do we react with fear, isolation and self-doubt, or find the wherewithal to respond with hope, empathy and self-worth that enables a mindful, intentional and strategic response? In the story of now, the group is the protagonist, the one who enters the conflict and faces up to a test or task.

Ganz explained the challenge for any organizer or leader who wants to initiate change is to break through the "inertia of habit" and get people to pay attention, to motivate them to risk doing something new and uncertain. An urgent need, outrage or a sense of injustice can propel a breakthrough: "It's the contradiction between the world as it is and the world as it ought to be. Our experience of that tension can break through inertia and apathy."

When I asked Ganz why the climate change narrative failed, he explained that campaigners should always create a powerful sense of injustice, a need for immediate change, or as Dr. King described it, "the fierce urgency of now." But for urgent action to become real the sense of challenge must be combined with a sense of hope by describing a plausible pathway to action, a credible path forward that makes strategic sense. When Ganz talks of hope he is not referring to some abstract dream of a better day. The goal needs to be specific and particular.

For instance, when he was trying to help farm workers years ago, Ganz spoke about justice for farm workers and the need for a farm workers' union, but since getting the employers to recognize such a union required boycotting their product (in this case grapes), achieving justice for farm workers boiled down to "don't eat a grape, don't buy a grape, get those grapes out of the stores." That was strategic and symbolic, and people made the connection. It was what Gandhi did in his Salt March through India. Martin Luther King did the same thing with bus seats, and the American Revolution of the 18th century used tea. But the end of Al Gore's film *An Inconvenient*

Truth offered 53 things that you could do. Too much information "trivialized the message." And none seemed linked to a focused strategy that offered a plausible pathway to success.

The emotional dissonance that arises from awareness of an injustice can motivate people to act, but not if it is linked with despair. "When anxiety hits and you're down in despair, then fear hits. You withdraw or strike out, neither of which helps to deal with the problem. But if you're up in hope or enthusiasm, you're more likely to ask questions and learn what you need to learn to deal with the unexpected," Ganz warned. "Leaders and organizers grapple all the time with how to create the tension to inspire a recognition of the need for change, which may incite anger, but also enough hope, empathy and self-worth so that the need for change translates into mindful action and not just reaction."

Ganz explained that a good story can help us not only understand the plot's lesson in our head, but feel it in our heart. When a story communicates courage, fear, hope, anxiety or exhilaration, we can feel it and understand the lesson not just conceptually. We grasp it emotionally, and the story's moral teaching, both cognitive and emotional, helps equip us to deal with our own challenging choices. Faith traditions, family traditions, cultural traditions are best taught through stories, he said: "This is a critical form of empowering discourse. It's how we learn to be change agents."

He stressed that relationships are built through narratives and shared commitments, but if a leader only creates anxiety, in an effort to communicate urgency and break through inertia, the result can be some form of despair or fear that doesn't spark action at all. So when telling a story of injustice or crisis a leader must also weave a message of hope, evoke an experience of possibility, of empathy, and one's own self worth. Hope allows us to be creative problem solvers, and it helps to counterbalance anxiety. "It is one of the most precious gifts we can give each other and the people we work with."

Ganz told me that a challenge and quest for hope and courage is found in the celebrated Saint Crispin's Day speech in Shakespeare's

play *Henry V*. Here the young king is motivating his troops before
the Battle of Agincourt. His army is grossly outnumbered and exhausted; the odds are fearful and their opponents are fresh. Henry
explains that anyone who wants to leave can go, he would not die
in that man's company, but for those who stay—"We few, we happy
few, we band of brothers"—the king promises an opportunity for
immortality. Ganz loves this speech because King Henry never talks
about victory and never even mentions the French. His call to arms
is purely about who we are and what our values call us to do. It's
about possibilities. "It is a moment when we can grasp the meaning
of our lives and our deaths," said Ganz, who adds its brilliance also
lies in the way Shakespeare showed us how to restore agency and
value to people who are utterly despairing. It's a prototypical locker
room speech that doesn't demonize opponents or even mention victory, yet it speaks to the core of its audience and explains what gives
meaning to their lives.

A public narrative is a call to action. Its story is built around a
shared challenge, the choice that must be made in response to that
threat, and an outcome that conveys a moral. Ganz offered a simple
and contemporary analogy: Being asked to change one wasteful light
bulb is one thing, "but ask me to help persuade all of the Kennedy
School to change all of its light bulbs by signing a student petition,
joining a delegation to the dean and adding my name to a public list
of students committed to changing the light bulbs where they live,"
now that's a call to arms. Even if the possibility of success seems
remote, this is a story that offers a credible path and specific action.

Stories not only teach us how to act, they also inspire us to take
action, and Ganz detailed how a compelling narrative is crafted with
three essential elements: plot, character and moral. *Plot* engages us,
captures our interest and moves us toward a goal. It becomes exciting
when there are unexpected twists and turns. We listen with greater
attention to the storyteller when something surprises us, when the
unknown intervenes. It doesn't have to be a gut-wrenching calamity

or a dangerous predicament, but when a suspenseful challenge looms we are intrigued.

This is where the protagonist must figure out what to do, and we become engrossed and involved in their *character* as they make a critical choice. For the story to have power it must draw us in emotionally, so we can identify empathetically with the character, so we feel and see through their eyes. Up until this point the story may have been boring, but suddenly we all lean forward, we're all ears. Why do we care? Because we have all had to face the unknown and make choices, and at the core of the human condition—ours and the character's—is agency and choice.

The story's conclusion needs to have a *moral* that brings us greater understanding, something to live by, a lesson of the heart as well as the head, Ganz said. The memory of a favorite book or film stays with us for years or decades because we can still feel the pull of emotion and the moral universe that created it. "We experience the emotional content, not just the intellectual takeaway. A story teaches us a moral. How did the protagonist access those emotional resources? How did they find courage? How did they find hope? It turns out we're incredibly curious about that."

Stories also show us how to manage our lives, face difficulties and rise above stressful situations in unfamiliar circumstances, and while outcomes may be uncertain, we gain strength and hope from watching a hero face those challenges and navigate through rough waters. Dealing with fear is a central moral question, as is the question of how to learn through empathy. This shared wisdom, and uplifting of positive values, is what makes a ripping biography so difficult to put down, and it is achieved through the language of emotion, not through vague, intellectual abstractions.

People are often reluctant to share their stories because they think their own experiences are too trivial or don't matter, but that is not true, especially in the public domain. Everyone has a story, "and you have a responsibility to offer a public account of who you are, why you do what you do, and where you hope to lead." Ganz referred to a Yiddish riddle that asks, Who discovered water? The answer is, I don't know, but it wasn't a fish. The point is, we are all fish in our own experience, and we can't see beyond our own little ponds.

Whenever Ganz coaches people in developing their stories, the first thing they usually say is nothing dramatic ever happened to them. So he asks: Have you experienced pain or loss? Did you ever find hope? When you start digging, you find the experiential foundation that enables a person to communicate something real about themselves, Ganz said.

The Harvard expert said such stories are never trivial, never irrelevant, which is why parents of small children spend a lot of time telling stories. Are they doing this simply to entertain them? No. Storytelling sessions are instructions in agency, in how to access the emotional resources we will all need later in life, to make the right choices. It's value teaching, and children crave this.

Narratives provide information that both children and adults need in order to make judgments. "We're just beginning to actually understand these processes that have been known to religious leaders for thousands of years," said Ganz. So let's build hope instead of fear, empathy instead of alienation, people's sense of self-worth rather than their sense of inadequacy. The current oversupply of scientific information often increases that sense of inadequacy: "Economists do that very successfully. They've mystified the whole debate about economics."

Good leaders understand a story must always be very specific and evoke a particular time and mood. It should be framed in a vibrant setting, with bright color, flavor and gritty texture. The more detail the teller paints into a picture, the more effectively the canvas communicates feelings, values and morals. Paradoxically, Ganz pointed out that the more specific and detailed a story is, the more universal it becomes and the greater its connection to us all.

Skilled public narrative is an essential element in leadership, especially when the public square is filled with PR, mistrust and disinterest. As we have seen all through this book, presenting people with a barrage of facts and evidence that stirs up feelings of guilt and fear is not enough. Virtually everyone I interviewed had concerns about the poor quality of environmental narrative and how a lack of storytelling facility leads to greater public anxiety and inaction.

Marshall Ganz brilliantly details how to craft a public story that can deliver really bad news about a problem while it offers a level of hopefulness that rises above any anxiety created by a deeper under-standing of a problem. Such a story becomes an emotional dialogue that speaks about deeply held values, about an inspired future that is hopeful and steeped in those values.

SECTION F

From the Heart

20

The Golden Rule

with KAREN ARMSTRONG and JOAN HALIFAX

PRIZE-WINNING BRITISH scholar Karen Armstrong has spent most of her life delving into the history and mystery of the world's great religions. In 1984 she was assigned to write and present a television documentary focusing on the life of Saint Paul, and while retracing his steps in the Holy Land, Armstrong's own life found a new direction. Absorbed in discovering similarities and connections between religions, she began delving into the history of such traditions and made history herself by winning the TED prize in 2008. TED Talks—a lecture series named for Technology, Entertainment and Design—named her as its most exceptional speaker that year, and she used her $100,000 award to spearhead the creation of a Charter for Compassion.[1]

"When you win the TED prize, they give you a wish for a better world, which they then try to make happen. I felt that what was needed from my field was a greater emphasis on compassion," Karen Armstrong explained.[2] This is what all the great world traditions insist is at the center of the religious life, and compassion is the test of true spirituality. We rarely hear about it, yet our "paramount duty" is to respect our fellow human beings. Compassion is a virtuous cycle, and practicing the Golden Rule yields an expanded sense of self, which yields ever more compassionate behavior.

Armstrong's research has shown that although ancient sages, philosophers and religious leaders such as Confucius, Socrates and Buddha may have come from different traditions, they all advanced a practical message for everyday life. The Chinese philosopher Confucius, who lived from 551–479 BCE, is said to have been the first person to formulate the Golden Rule: Do not do to others that which we do not want them to do to us. The book of Leviticus, written circa 1400 BCE, said, "Love thy neighbor as thyself." Similar statements are found in Taoism, Buddhism, Hinduism and many other religions and philosophies.

Religious knowledge is meant to be practical, Armstrong stressed, although in the West and in this modern era, people get hung up on doctrines and beliefs that become a kind of "head trip." Traditionally, religion is about changing behavior in a way that changes an individual at a profound level. One of the chief obstacles to enlightenment is selfishness and egotism, and compassion is the surest way to move beyond the ego. "You have to dethrone yourself from the center of your world and put another there." When the disciples of Confucius asked which of his teachings could be put into practice all day, every day, his answer was simple: *shu*. This means to "look into your own heart, discover what gives you pain, then refuse under any circumstances whatsoever to inflict that pain on anybody else."

Confucius said that practicing this all day, every day—not just when you feel like it—leads to an ecstasy of stepping outside the self, and gradually this becomes the path to enlightenment and enhancement of being. When asked how to apply this in political life, Confucius said that when among the common people, you must behave as though you were in the presence of an important guest. If you seek to establish yourself politically and economically, then seek to establish others. In Buddhist terminology this means taking responsibility for the pain you see in the world, not dismissing it or thinking it is not your concern. It means active concern for others.

American Zen Buddhist and teacher Joan Halifax explained to me that it is possible to train in the processes that precede compas-

**Look into your own heart, discover what gives you pain,
then refuse under any circumstances whatsoever
to inflict that pain on anybody else. Never treat others
as you would not like to be treated yourself.**

KAREN ARMSTRONG

sion. This includes practicing the capacities for balanced attention, for positive regard and unselfish motivation: "If you tend to be a reactive person, you can start to see and feel your own reactivity when it arises and turn that dial down. Other aspects include cultivating a moral and ethical sensitivity so that we operate responsibly in the world around us and are not attached to any outcome. Another quality to cultivate is intention, as in, How can I serve here? What needs to happen? What will reduce suffering?"[3]

I told Karen Armstrong that people in Canada's environmental community are angry about the lack of action on climate change and frustrated by the resistance of governments and business leaders. It appears activists are unreceptive to the message of compassion, because it seems passive and they have made a moral choice not to be bystanders.

Armstrong said compassion may seem like an idealistic pursuit, far removed from the realities of life today, but she was quick to explain that the great sages who preached compassion didn't live in caves. They lived in extremely violent societies, like our own, where "aggression had reached an unprecedented crescendo." During the era of Confucius, for instance, all the Chinese states embarked upon a fight that lasted two centuries, until only one was left and became the Chinese Empire. "The loss of life, destruction of property and the environment was absolutely appalling."

Ours is an equally threatened world in many ways, and if we persist along our present course we may not survive. The most important path to change is to treat one another with absolute respect.

The historian went on to say it is important to speak out against injustice, "but to be effective you must ask yourself, are your actions about your ego and punishing your opponent or are they about real change?" If you come from an antagonistic, egotistical position, people will double down and resist what you are trying to achieve. This is why advocates and other public figures need to develop self-discipline and self-awareness. "They need to realize that the pain and fear motivating their anger is the same pain and fear motivating their opponents to deny this horrendous scenario."

Gandhi is an obvious example of someone who was working in an extremely difficult environment, but he refused to condemn the British. He was not averse to speaking out, but he urged his followers to always ask themselves whether they were speaking out to punish rather than to ameliorate the situation.

Armstrong is fond of quoting Saint Paul, who included a hymn to charity in his letter to the Corinthians: "Charity is patient, is kind. It is not puffed up." He also noted, "Charity takes no delight in the wrongdoing of others."[4] Very often when people are protesting against an injustice, they become puffed up with self-righteous indignation. This will get you nowhere. Armstrong admonished us always ask ourselves, Are we seeking to make a difference? Or do we simply want to let off steam?

Armstrong's work often deals with acrimonious individuals, and in her studies of fundamentalist religions she has found that every militant religious movement has a profound fear of annihilation in its origins. "They believe, even in the United States, that modern, liberal or secular ideologues want to wipe them out." When people feel their backs are to the wall, they lash out violently. If any movement is attacked aggressively, their members invariably become more extreme.

When it comes to the environment, Armstrong suggested that much of the denial that results from public debate is rooted in fear and dread, because change means doing away with a lot of material comforts on which people have come to depend. We, especially in the Western world, have become "absolutely spoiled and selfish," and people in a materialistic culture cling to their possessions because they have no psychological resources to deal with scarcity. The idea of giving things up, of not having a warm house or not being able to jump into our cars every time we need to, bewilders and paralyzes people. "The scale of what is required if we are to meet this challenge is monumental, and so some people say it isn't happening, it's all nonsense." Instead of yelling at people and being inimical, which simply makes them more paralyzed, Armstrong suggested that activists must try to gently guide one another out of that paralysis. Our best hope is to share each other's pain, dial down the heated discussions so we can all realize we are on the brink of situations that are unprecedented in human history.

How do we achieve a sustainable environment? This is something none of us has a full answer to yet. If we think we have all the answers we are deceiving ourselves. The situation is exacerbated by a plethora of social and political problems. People in developing countries ask why they should hold back on industrial growth and continue living in poverty when those in the West enjoy much better living conditions. We've got to sit down quietly together, face the problems, find solutions, and learn to live with a new reality, said Armstrong.

And what is required of us all—whether we are trying to decrease the threat of terrorism or create a viable environment—is a spiritual revival. That doesn't mean we should all go off and say our prayers, Armstrong commented. People who think that have adopted the modern, reductive way of thinking about religion. Instead, spiritual revival "means that we have to do a lot of work on our own internal selves, so that we are ready to make sacrifices, to give up comforts, to cut down on our travel."

This asks an awful lot from people. It's asking them to make massive sacrifices, and not everyone can do that just by thinking about it rationally. "You need to dissuade these fears and not present people with a world of stark terror, which makes them batten down the hatches. Do it in a way that allows them to start thinking: How am I going to live without my motor car?"

During the financial crisis in 2008 many business people gazed into an abyss and realized what can happen when greed takes over. Greed is helping to destroy our environment, through our lust for material consumption, our desire for luxury, warmth and travel—doing whatever we like without being accountable. But it's not too late. People such as Buddha and Confucius are remembered to this day because they changed the world by changing the way people thought and acted. Kings and important businesspeople who were alive at that time are long forgotten, but the Buddha founded one of the oldest and most enduring institutions in all of world history.

21

Speak the Truth,
But Not to Punish

with THICH NHAT HANH

A COUPLE OF YEARS AGO, my wife Enid and I participated in a five-day program at the University of British Columbia with the renowned Vietnamese monk Thich Nhat Hanh.

"As activists we want to do something to help the world to suffer less," Thich Nhat Hanh said, but when we're not peaceful, when we don't have enough compassion in us, we are unable to do much to help the world. "Peace, love, and happiness must always begin in us, with ourselves first. There is suffering, fear, and anger inside of us, and when we take care of it, we are taking care of the world."[1]

Thich Nhat Hanh used the example of a pine tree and suggested, what if that tree asked us what it could do to help the world? Our answer would be very clear: "You should be a beautiful, healthy pine tree. You help the world by being your best." That is true for humans also. The most basic thing we can do to help the world is to be healthy, solid, loving, and gentle to ourselves. Then when people look at us, they will gain confidence and say, If he or she can do that, I can too. So anything you do for yourself, you do for the world, he said. "Don't think that you and the world are two separate things. When you breathe in mindfully and gently, when you feel the wonder of being alive, remember that you're also doing this for the world. Practicing with that kind of insight, you will succeed in helping the world. You don't have to wait until tomorrow. You can do it right now."

During the retreat, lectures invariably touched on the subject of anger, and I listened as he encouraged me to examine the anger I felt toward special interests that mislead the public about the environmental challenges we face. One day Thich Nhat Hanh told us Buddha's story of the second arrow: When an arrow strikes you there is pain, but if a second arrow drives into the same spot, the pain is excruciating, much worse. The Buddha advised when you have pain in your body or your mind, breathe in and out and recognize the significance of the pain but don't exaggerate its importance. If you are full of anger, worry and fear over the pain you magnify the suffering. This is the second arrow—and it is directed from within.

The Buddha proposed many ways to practice reducing pain in our bodies and in our emotions, to become reconciled within ourselves. Pain increases as tension increases, and it can be reduced when we release the tension. The monk said that this can be done while lying, sitting or walking. "Walk like a free person.… The skill we need is how to lay down our burden in order to be light. The Buddha said that you shouldn't amplify your pain by exaggerating the situation.… So when you experience pain, whether physical or mental, you have to recognize it just as it is and not exaggerate it…When you can make peace with it, you won't suffer as much." When we get angry and revolt against something, when we worry too much and imagine we are going to die soon, our pain is multiplied 100 times. "That is the second arrow."

If we want to help the environment suffer less, we have to reduce the suffering in ourselves, Thich Nhat Hanh explained simply. "Be loving, and gentle to yourself." Avoid the second arrow. He talked about a heart of understanding that is beyond intellect, that is discovered by looking so deeply we touch the seed of understanding and compassion within. Compassion can neutralize anger and hate, and meditation can burn away afflictions such as fear, despair and delusion. "Deep meditation helps us transcend the notion of being

There is suffering, fear,
and anger inside of us,
and when we take care of it,
we are taking care of the world.

THICH NHAT HANH

and non-being. Nirvana is not a place we will arrive at in the future, but the nature of reality."

He suggested we should listen more deeply, and allow others to speak as this helps to reduce their suffering. "Water the seeds of compassion; don't water the seeds of anger and hatred." Use non-accusatory language so it is easier for others to hear our message. Effective listening does not involve hearing something and comparing that information with our own views. We learn nothing from such an exchange.

Grassroots success is effective and possible only if activists and leaders first deal with their own anger and fear. Spiritual practice is needed to transform society and give courage to leaders so they will speak out. He said a mother would die for her children because of her great love, and similarly, if a person has great compassion they will not fear being ostracized or ridiculed if they decide to challenge the status quo.

I had been asked to moderate a conversation between David Suzuki and Thich Nhat Hanh. The day of our taped interview, following the five-day course at UBC, started with an extraordinary experience. Thich Nhat Hanh arrived at the pre-arranged location while David Suzuki and I were in another part of the building, so someone quickly found us and explained that the famous monk had gone for a walk in the garden. We rushed to catch up with his small group and strolled about 20 paces behind. Walking in this peaceful space, he touched some of the flowers with great tenderness, and as I watched, the garden became intensely green. As the monk was appreciating each flower, petal and leaf, Suzuki leaned over and said softly, "Do you know what I see? I see photosynthesis: the sun pouring down, creating energy, turning it into all this green, all these plants that allow us to breathe."

The conversation began when I asked for Thich Nhat Hanh's reaction to a 1930 statement made by a Wall Street banker: "People need to be trained to desire, to want new things, even before the old things have been entirely consumed. Man's desires must overshadow his needs."[2]

I was expecting an answer about consumerism and the destructiveness of clinging, but he gently turned the conversation in an unexpected direction by saying how the desire for more can be a deep and noble desire in each human being. "Like the desire to love, to protect, to help, to serve, the desire to be loved, to understand, to learn. These are very deep desires in each human being, in every one of us, and you cannot set a limit on that kind of desire.... You can continue to learn, to understand more about yourself, about the world outside you. You can continue to develop your love into the infinite. In Buddhism we say that love is something that has no frontiers."

I asked how we can bring about the collective awakening needed to stop destroying our planet, and Thich Nhat Hanh told the story of a similar longing for change in a five- or six-year-old child who stood up in front of a large audience in Plum Village (the spiritual community he founded in France) and asked why his father continued to smoke, knowing it was not good for him. "That [wanting change] is a theme, a subject of meditation, and I think if we can answer that question we will have a lot of insight about how to handle the situation of our planet. It's very difficult to offer an answer to the child if you do not have the time to look deeply into the situation." But Thich Nhat Hanh told the child that in order to stop smoking the father must feel his child's love: "Your love will be an important force in order to help him to stop."

During our UBC interview, Thich Nhat Hanh said we must build communities that model how to live sustainably, and that requires inspirational, confident leadership. Vancouver mayor Gregor Robertson said it was a compelling concept, but the challenge is how to reach consensus for a higher-level commitment in a city that is a very culturally and politically diverse community. He added that politicians are often criticized for trying to set big goals, such as ending homelessness or becoming the greenest city in the world. Robertson said many citizens are disillusioned with issues of climate change and poverty.

The monk explained that people should remind each other that this is the way of life that guarantees a future. Senior members of the community—the mayor, city council, people in government—should set an example and show people "that they are abiding by the spirit and the way. I think it's very important." He said citizens should vote only for those who adopt the kind of lifestyle that sets an example to inspire hope and confidence. Leaders should be people who not only have the talent to run the country's business but also represent our global ethics.

Feelings of despair must be dealt with, because they overwhelm and paralyze people, said Thich Nhat Hanh; he added that this is a key reason why people do not respond to the threat of global warming, despite mounting and devastating evidence. They cannot raise themselves out of the pit of despair, let alone save the world. "Despair is growing in our society, and because of that we feel helpless. We don't believe that we can do anything to reverse the situation. Again, I think community building is very important, to show people that living simply and happily is possible." When we understand the interconnectedness of all life, when we recognize we are not separate, we can expand our compassion and ourselves so that we embrace Earth and protect it.

The monk said that people are deluded into thinking fame, power, wealth or sex will bring them happiness, and these become refuges from the truth and challenges facing Mother Earth. Today's addiction to consumerism and a frantic lifestyle is a mask behind which people hide their emotional and spiritual wounds. It provides only a temporary respite from fear and unhappiness: "They suffer deeply even if they have a lot of these kinds of things. Many of them commit suicide." Without love, brotherhood and sisterhood, people destroy themselves, and Thich Nhat Hanh urged people to step onto the path of love and understanding if they want to find the strength to let go of the mask and awaken to reality.

A life of consumerism is not life. "We have to help people learn how to live again. We just sit down and breathe and enjoy each other." He said this is one of the best moments of a retreat: when people don't consume anything, don't have music, don't have sound, don't have alcohol, don't have anything but a chance to sit and enjoy each others' presence. He said everyone knows how to breathe, to appreciate they are alive on this beautiful planet, and that can bring joy. "So we have to educate our citizens to see that happiness does not lie in consumption but lies in the fact that you are free enough: You have enough time to enjoy yourself, to enjoy each other, to enjoy the environment."

The simple acts of life are treasures, and we should savor them, knowing everything we need to be happy is right here, right now. "In the Buddhist tradition we have a practice like a tea ceremony. We just have one cup of tea but we spend one hour and a half together. Why do we need one hour and a half in order to enjoy a cup of tea? Because the tea ceremony is an art. If you know how to sit, how to breathe, how to look, how to listen and how to be together, that ceremony can bring a lot of joy. And you don't consume much, one cup only. We have lost our capacity of being happy, because we are so busy. And busy in what? Busy trying to cover up the suffering inside."

I mentioned that there are climate scientists and political leaders who want to do something positive about climate change but have a difficult time because so many people stir up mischief about these issues. When the public is misinformed and unaware that a problem exists, it's very difficult for leaders to lead, I said, and while I understood what he said about community building and agreed that is a the solution, I explained I still worry about taking our eyes off the people who are up to mischief on larger levels.

This took us directly back to the issue of despair, and Thich Nhat Hanh said if we don't deal with despair the situation will get worse. "We have to accept this civilization can be destroyed, not by something outside, but by ourselves. Many civilizations have been destroyed in the past, and to accept that can only be helpful, and it may give us a sense of peace so we can become a better worker for the environment." He said that many people know what is happening but do nothing because they are just trying to survive. "If you help them to sort out the inside, you can help them to have hope, to have peace in themselves and suddenly they have the strength to come back to themselves...and that person could be an instrument for the protection of the environment."

During our interview David Suzuki asked if accepting the reality that this could all end disastrously means we retreat into passivity.

Thich Nhat Hanh said a century or two is nothing in geological terms. "This civilization might be destroyed, and it may take a billion years more in order to have another civilization. That already happened in the past. We have to accept reality, and acceptance like that can bring us peace. And with that kind of peace, we have force and it can flow, and it can reverse the situation. Meditation plays a role." He said that to meditate means to look deeply, and by looking deeply we have insight, which frees us from despair and anger. This allows us to become a better worker for the environment.

Suzuki added that he understood the cycles of extinction of species, as a natural part of evolution. Species become extinct as conditions change, and new species evolve, "but many of us have children and grandchildren who are precious, and when we see the approaching calamity it is difficult to accept." Again Thich Nhat Hanh stressed the importance of building community and living in a way that can become a model for others. "If everyone can live like that, truly there will be a future for our children. Our society needs a lot of healing and this is not possible without a good environment. That's why, when building a community, you build also an environment where you can see hope, brotherhood, sisterhood and a future."

He said we should bring a spiritual dimension to the work of protecting the environment. "The role of meditation, the role of community building, the role of healing and transforming in our daily life is crucial for the environment. You cannot just have projects and initiatives without taking care of the suffering inside." At the end of our interview I was worried that Thich Nhat Hanh had been saying that we should simply withdraw and meditate, so I mentioned that one of his monks had told me his Bay Nha monastery in the central highlands of Vietnam had placed pictures on its website of bad police who were abusing monks and nuns. I pointed out that this seemed like the strategy of activists. Was he saying we should not be activists?

He looked at me in a quiet, piercing way that stopped my breath, and said slowly: "Speak the truth, but not to punish." It took me some time to realize that I had been given a Zen koan[3] by one of the most important Zen masters of our generation. I've been thinking about it ever since. It was the most profound moment of this entire three-year journey of research and writing, the seminal moment, because it gathered together the deepest voices and most profound threads of this long book into one elegant sentence.

Understanding this koan is a work in progress for me but the more I ponder it, the more it seems to be about balance, speaking up against injustice with courage and passion but with greater awareness of the dangers in becoming overly adversarial and treating those who disagree as foes.

It is important to educate the public about the PR campaigns written about earlier in this book, but it is equally important to ensure, as Rabbi Hillel encouraged, that our argument is for the sake of heaven. We must be willing to stand in the shoes of others if we are to debate controversial issues with equanimity and avoid gridlock.

Thich Nhat Hanh's koan brought me back to his advice to hold our anger with an energy of mindfulness, like the sun shining upon a flower, penetrating deeply until the petals open. Anger can give us the mettle to speak with courage and conviction, but also the venom that blinds us to the views of others.

22

We Need Warmheartedness

with THE 14TH DALAI LAMA

THE TIBETAN PLATEAU has often been referred to as the roof of
the world because it stretches over a vast area with an elevation
averaging more than three miles above sea level. This magnificent
region—larger in size than France, Spain, Germany and Italy combined—brings life-giving nourishment to almost 40 percent of the
world's population.

Its glaciers, located northeast of the Himalayas, have been described as the water tower of India and China because this icy realm
holds the third largest reservoir of freshwater on Earth, outside the
North and South Poles. The Tibetan plateau, of which the autono-
mous region of Tibet covers about half, is the birthplace of four of
the world's great rivers—the Yangtze, Mekong, Yellow and Brahmaputra—and many others, including the Indus and Salween.[1]

Climate change is visible to the naked eye in Tibet. "Temperatures are rising four times faster than elsewhere in China, and the
Tibetan glaciers are retreating at a higher speed than in any other
part of the world," said glaciologist Qin Dahe, former head of the
China Meteorological Administration. He said this catastrophe is
causing floods and mudflows in the short term, and in the long term

the melting will affect vital Asian lifelines such as the Indus and Ganges. "Once they vanish, water supplies in those regions will be in peril."[2]

Recent research by experts at NASA and the Chinese Academy of Sciences shows that the black carbon being deposited on these glaciers, generated from industrial production in South Asia, is accelerating shrinking. Soot absorbs incoming solar radiation and speeds melting, and it's helping to turn the world's largest non-polar ice masses into what has been described as a climate change hot spot.[3]

I first traveled to Tibet in 2003. Our group, including former Canadian cabinet minister Flora MacDonald, toured for two weeks with naturalists, community organizers and one of the world's leading ornithologists. We were looking into primary healthcare and environmental sustainability projects being led by Future Generations in villages across Tibet, and our host was the founder of that group, Daniel Taylor. He had invited the David Suzuki Foundation to become involved in Future Generations' Four Great Rivers Project in eastern Tibet.[3]

Future Generations was promoting community-led development and helping create a conservation zone in the southeastern part of Tibet, to protect 46 million acres of biodiversity. The Chinese government had started to reevaluate the massive amount of trees being cut down in what is now designated the Four Great Rivers Protection Area, and we were helping them better understand sustainable land-use planning and resource management.

I learned how deforestation in Tibet was affecting the Yangtze River region, an area that suffered some of the worst flooding in half a century during a disastrous 1998 event that resulted in 15 million homeless and an economic loss of $26 billion.[4]

Our trip to Tibet was capped off with a drive down the treacherous Friendship Highway to Kathmandu. We passed many beautiful sites and a mixture of fear and weather—starting with a snowfall on an 18,000-foot mountain pass—sometimes deterred us from seeing all the sacred sites we would have liked. But on our descent we managed to visit a cave of revered Tibetan saint Milarepa, who is said to have concentrated so intensely one day that he levitated its massive stone roof. We also visited Rombuk Monastery, the highest monastery in the world at 16,300 feet (near the base of Mt. Everest), and, because we were with Flora, we privately toured the Jokhang Temple in Lhasa, holiest site in Tibetan Buddhism.

I visited Tibet again in 2006, to evaluate and report on the progress of our joint conservation project.

Important work continued for about five years in this botanical treasure trove, which boasts some of the world's deepest, steepest river valleys (such as the Brahmaputra gorge—four times deeper than the Grand Canyon) and features climate zones ranging from tropical to polar. We were training villagers as caregivers in health and hygiene, developing leaders in ecosystem-based land-use planning. It is the kind of environmental work that is bottom up, not paternalistic in the sense of being directed from the top down or from outside the region.

Back in Tibet, we toured the Four Great Rivers area and drove for five days off-road to the base of Mt. Kailash, which we circumnavigated on foot. Here I saw the spirituality of the people but also how little Tibetans have, how rudimentary their lives are, how arid the landscape is—and how perilously close they live to the edge.

At one point we stopped for a break under some trees and I saw a young boy selling some dismal looking apples. The Good Samaritan in me said I should buy all his apples for far more than he was asking. As I walked back to the car, feeling very content and thinking he would be shocked at what he received for his apples, my wife, Enid, was yelling out the window, "Give him back his bowl, give him back his bowl." Turning around, I saw a woeful look on his face and rushed to return his precious bowl. Suddenly his face lit up in a huge smile as happiness was restored. I don't know exactly how many bowls I have in my house, but obviously far more than I need. That was a big lesson for me, from a small boy, and my wife.

We have such abundance in Canada, yet everything at this high elevation in Tibet seemed brighter, more saturated with color, more vividly intense. The sky was bluer, the snow was whiter and the feeling of connection was stronger too. Gazing at the peak of Mt. Everest, you see it pierce the jet stream's river of wind that streaks around the globe at high speed, and you see how it stitches together Earth and sky.

Once, on our way to hike around Mt. Kailash, when we were days away from any town or sustained light, I stepped outside the little pup tent in the middle of the night. Everything around me was pitch black, but it seemed the stars were right beside me, not just above. I could see the depth of the Milky Way, almost touch the constellations, and everything was so close I felt completely connected with the stars.

Tibet offers an acute lesson in interconnectedness that is hard to miss when you're there. Tibet showed me precisely how an area can suffer when climate change is on fast forward. I also realized how vulnerable its people are. Sometimes we would pass through a village where everyone was outside trying to plant trees in what looked like desert to us. Traveling to Tibet was like visiting a canary in a coal mine, tracking a sensitive indicator that's issuing an early warning of great danger.

In 2011 I traveled to Dharamshala—home of the 14th Dalai Lama and headquarters of the Tibetan government in exile—for the 23rd Mind Life Conference,[5] a five-day discussion about the environmental crisis, ecology and ethics of climate change. Meetings were held in the Dalai Lama's house, and speakers included public intellectuals such as Sallie McFague, Elke Weber, Joan Halifax and Daniel Goleman.

During this conference I spoke with His Holiness privately, and that intensely moving interview was one of the first I did for this book. Although our conversation took place years ago, I believe the Dalai Lama's thoughts and words are most fitting at the end of this long project.

His Holiness said, "The environment issue is most serious, the topmost importance. Billions of lives depend on the major rivers, which ultimately come from the Tibetan plateau. So it is very, very serious."[7] He made a surprisingly strong suggestion about Beijing, noting that the political agendas revolving around Tibet should be shelved for the time being so that the international community can focus on the impact of climate change on the plateau.

"If the Chinese leaders could look at the Tibet issue more realistically, then within a few days we can solve. But once environmental damage is done, it is impossible to change. Damage has already been done there. The repercussions will remain for decades, and in some cases cannot be reversed. So the political problem can wait another five years, 10 years, 50 years. We can wait. But the environment issue can't wait. Every month some more damage is done due to mining or deforestation. It has already happened like that."

His Holiness said it is our responsibility to raise awareness in people's minds because everyone should know of this crisis, and that people are suffering. Corruption is at the root of the issue: "It is like a new disease, a cancer on the whole planet, the whole humanity. What is wrong? Not a lack of judicial system, police force or government organization, but ultimately a lack of ethics and self-discipline. We should be thinking: I am a human being. I should not do this, for my own reputation, for my own interest, my own health, my family's well-being. We have a moral responsibility to make this known."

The spiritual, and secular leader talked about communicating the information frequently and clearly, saying that for 40 years he has been repeating his message of compassion. "Since 1973. I would repeat this a thousand times, seeing some effect. Whether people listen seriously or not, I continuously repeat that."

So I asked, do we simply ignore the propaganda and repeat the message? "Oh yes. Yes. Talk continuously," he said with a smile. "That is the main thing. I am always mentioning a Tibetan saying: Nine times failure, then nine times effort. This means effort, fail, again effort, again fail, again effort." He said people today want immediate results, and if we fail they give up and stop trying, "That's wrong. That is defeat."

He punctuated his remark by pointing a finger at my forehead, almost touching my brow. And then came one of the most profound moments for me through this entire journey, through all the interviews I have subsequently done for this book. It was the emotional, straight-to-the-heart message that spun me around and sent me down a different path of understanding, connecting and communicating.

The Dalai Lama said, "I think you acknowledge sometimes the Western brain looks more sophisticated, but in Tibet we operate from the heart and this is very strong. So combine these two, Asian heart and Western mind, and then we will have real success. Real success."

His Holiness planted the seed for a different kind of book, one that would look at the causes of miscommunication, mistrust and propaganda, but also look at educating the heart. He explained that warmheartedness extends to us all, to the planet, the ecology, and it is at the root of solving this ethical problem. Rather than anger, fear, suspicion and distrust, we need warmheartedness.

During one of the sessions in Dharamsala, His Holiness said that warmheartedness comes from the genuine practice of love, genuine compassion, genuine friendship and a genuine concern for the well-being of others. "We must respect all different forms of life, with less concern for getting something back." Genuine friendship is not based on money, education or knowledge and "because of human intelligence we understand the deeper meaning of reality, beyond biological factors."

The Dalai Lama's message connects with the comments of cognitive scientist George Lakoff (that facts alone don't change minds) and with the emotional dialogue lessons of Marshall Ganz. A search for answers in this new direction led me to interview Joel Bakan (who discussed the corruption and the human impact of

**I think you acknowledge sometimes
the Western brain looks more sophisticated,
but in Tibet we operate from the heart
and this is very strong. So combine these two,
Asian heart and Western mind, and
then we will have real success. Real success.**

THE 14TH DALAI LAMA

unfettered capitalism) and Dan Kahan (who explained how trust networks inform public opinion).

Writing *I'm Right* led to a much larger consideration about why we feel disconnected, disengaged, hopeless or frightened. Why are we gullible and why do we fail to act? The Dalai Lama has said we are raising a generation of passive bystanders, but why is that? These questions led me to interview people such as Carol Tavris, Jason Stanley and French philosopher Bruno Latour.

"When I came from Tibet in 1959 I had a shock," the Dalai Lama told our group at the outset of the Mind Life Conference. "In Tibet, everywhere there is very clean water, clean and pure. You can drink, enjoy. Only after I came outside Tibet, was the first time I heard, 'this water you cannot drink.' And I was very surprised. In Tibet there was no such thing." He said we are all aware of issues such as this now, and we should be deeply concerned because "it is a question of survival, not of me, not of 200 people, but of nearly seven billion people."

For this reason, he said, it is time to bring out the Western scientists, people with open, unbiased minds. He spoke of scientists as gurus, because they occupy a position of great authority in his view. "Through awareness, not meditation, we are learning. Through the help of scientists." And he stressed their message must be constant and clear, which led me to interview experts in deep listening skills

such as Otto Scharmer, social scientist Daniel Yankelovich and scenario planning guru Adam Kahane.

When the Dalai Lama explained that our problem with climate
change is about ethics, I started to ponder the moral imperative: It's
one thing to unknowingly harm someone but another altogether
to cause harm once you know damage is being done. There is an
obligation to stop. The great tragedy of climate change is, those who
will be harmed most are not those who are causing the problem.

During one of the sessions at the Dalai Lama's house, theologian
Sallie McFague said consumerism is going global, becoming a major
problem everywhere because of overconsumption and greed. "We
pretend we can hoard and gather more and more for ourselves, never
worrying about the rest. Science tells us we are interdependent and
interrelated whether we like it or not, but our culture fails to accept
this." She explained that happiness is found in self-emptying, not
filling up with material goods, but those of us who are well off and
have benefited tremendously from market capitalism don't want to
give up our privilege, "our exceptionalism." [8]

His Holiness emphasized that the real enemies are ignorance,
greed and lack of inner peace. "Physical things provide only physical comfort. Inner peace never comes from things. It comes from a
peaceful mind, a happy marriage, a healthy family and a warm heart.
These are key values. Taking care of physical comfort is just half."

He pointed out that we human beings have been blessed with a
keen brain that allows us to learn from the past and anticipate the
future. "Animals are just day by day, but we have this marvelous brain
that thinks in 10 years, 100 years, maybe 1,000 years. We human
beings have the ability to develop visions, and think long into the
future, this is our special quality, a gift from God, so we must use it.
If we are like animals then there is no hope.

"We also have a wonderful memory so we can record what happened. Only human beings know how to do this, maybe angels know
that too. We have the capacity, the ability, to look back several cen-

turies, and also think into the long future. With that ability we have to make a proper plan. Make constant tireless effort."

＊ ＊ ＊ ＊ ＊

My work takes place in the public square and involves interaction with lots of folks around the world with whom I consult, lecture and lead projects. During the journey of writing *I'm Right* I free-dived deeper than ever before into the realm of communication and came up almost breathless with new understandings about speaking from the heart. It's not good enough to be passionate about a subject, to feel strongly and speak loudly about it. To create powerful, persuasive narratives our starting point must be rooted in an attitude of empathy, respect, and compassion.

We are not going to change the world by yelling at people and telling them what to do—and that doesn't mean having to compromise on what is right, or tolerate corruption. We can make errors if we assume people are evil, just don't understand, don't have all the facts or are being apathetic; we need to recognize we can cause damage and add to the confusion if we hold fast to these attitudes. We become better ambassadors for the environment, or any cause, by putting ourselves in others' shoes. The lessons in this book are about the fundamentals of human relations—rooted in strength and compassion—or, as Adam Kahane said, power and love.

Toward the end of this journey I talked to Peter Senge about the idea of keeping an open mind and an open heart. We discussed how an open will is fundamental to human communications and human interaction. We spoke about cleaning up the inner ecology along with the outer, especially as it relates to how we collaborate on problems in the environment and pollution in the public square.

Senge is an expert on social systems dynamics who understands the undercurrents at play in all of us when we push hard with our own ideas, try to win an argument or convince somebody about something. This usually involves a pretty strong ego drive, and the ego is very sophisticated. It can disguise itself and convince us that the reason we're acting like a zealot is because we're right, we have the evidence and we are trying to save the world. But, he said, we become self-aware by asking ourselves from time to time, "Am I being effective in this situation? Are my inner needs getting in the way?".

All we really ever have is our own awareness, our own experience, and we all know that we're not as effective as we could or should be when our anger sometimes gets in the way. But if we become more disciplined in developing our awareness and compassion we are able to operate in a state of harmony and alignment, and ultimately become more effective communicators.

Peter Senge illustrated his point with an artistic metaphor. "I think all great artists have a deep understanding that they're on a very personal journey and that, paradoxically, it has nothing to do with them. Whether it's music, poetry or visual art doesn't matter. It comes through them. It doesn't come from them. There's a larger force or a larger reality that they're plugged into that is enabling their art to manifest. Artists understand that to be aware gives them a kind of a doorway into the larger reality."[9]

This paradox is very alive in a project like this book. Researching and writing it has been a deeply personal exploration, and yet the larger reality has little to do with me. When we are working with all our hearts for a cause, we are in a state of connection to something far beyond ourselves—like that night I stood on a dark Tibetan plateau and felt the stars shimmering all around me.

"The inner and the outer are dissolving; the inner and the outer start to dance," is how Senge described it. "Let's just say the boundary between the self and the larger world, the universe, has become more permeable." People talk about a calling—something you find you've just got to do—and perhaps this kind of passion shows up in our awareness when we are more connected, more in tune with some larger reality, and when we manage to connect the Western brain with the Tibetan heart.

Epilogue:
Lessons Learned

MY ORIGINAL INTEREST in writing this book began with David Suzuki's question: Why aren't people demanding action on environmental issues like climate change, despite the overwhelming evidence? This mission evolved along the way, and soon I was looking into the sorry state of public discourse regarding debates over everything from the safety of vaccines and gun control to refugee immigration. I also began questioning some of my own deepest values.

Suzuki's question, and what it reveals about our clumsy approach to public debate, also led me to the title of this book. *I'm Right* encapsulates much of what's wrong with our current approach to public conversations: our lack of reasonableness and empathy when dealing with those who disagree with us. Self-righteous attitudes get in the way of healthy public debate.

I focused on problems of never-ending polarization and explored the social and psychological factors that drive us to extremes and pollute the public square, but I also wanted to offer hopeful advice from this age of polluted discourse. During my research several key learnings and themes emerged, and I offer them here in summary.

✦ ✦ ✦ ✦ ✦

The first deals with the role of advocacy in public discourse: it can unintentionally create powerful barriers to change when it combines with forces of social psychology that close minds and drive unappealing levels of self-righteousness. Clearly an unyielding, one-sided attitude can create a mood of hostility and lead to polarization rather than change.

Stubborn adversarial advocacy dominates our society, and is coming from all sides. Regarding climate change, the resulting polarization is exacerbated by a scientific community that doesn't understand the rules of communication under conditions of political polarization. As a result, highly qualified and knowledgeable experts deliver scientific evidence to a public that is more mistrustful and inattentive than curious.

Daniel Yankelovich pointed out that advocacy has a valuable role to play—but combative, biased advocacy can also undermine public confidence and lead to paralysis just as quickly as institutional propaganda can. Unyielding, one-sided debates and non-stop controversy undermine society's ability to solve problems, and the noise stops people engaging because they feel hopeless and discouraged.

It is extremely difficult to break out of this advocacy trap, but as Roger Conner explained we can avoid stepping into it in the first place by adopting attitudes of respect, objectivity and fair-mindedness towards people we disagree with. Policing our own aggression helps open up space for real conversation.

Without a doubt, the world is a safer, healthier and more just place today thanks to advocates such as Henry David Thoreau, Martin Luther King and Gandhi, who struggled for civil and human rights, democracy, the environment and more. But advocacy can become a trap when groups view each other as not just wrong but as wrongdoers.

People don't start out mired in hostility. The situation evolves. When someone publicly disagrees with something we feel strongly about, we perceive them as aggressors and we begin to question their motives and intentions. When people criticize or condemn our cause or our reasoning, our defense mechanisms kick in. Anger simmers and escalates. When people on both sides of an argument draw their positions from the perceived bad behavior of the other, they eventually start treating each other as enemies, and this provokes a perpetual shoving match and eventual gridlock.

We need to recognize, as Roger Connor said, that few of us are truly evil—and that good people sometimes do bad things for good reasons. Carol Tavris echoed this, saying the greatest danger we face is not only from bad people doing corrupt and evil things, but also from good people who justify the bad and corrupt things they do in order to preserve their belief that they're good, kind and ethical.

Most of us consider ourselves to be reasonable and ethical, so when it's suggested that we are behaving unreasonably or unethically our self-image is threatened. That's when the powerful unconscious force of self-justification kicks in to reduce the unpleasant sting of cognitive dissonance, which arises when we know we have behaved badly. We work hard to defend our actions and maintain a favorable self-image, and sometimes we do this even when we harm others or are confronted by evidence that we are wrong. This self-deception is worse than lying, because it allows us to deceive ourselves and interferes with our ability to self-correct. The more time, effort, money and public face we attach to our decisions, the harder it is to admit we are wrong. Awareness of this inner conflict can enable us to turn down the static in our own interactions, and in the public square.

The forces of dissonance and self-justification help explain the unyielding one-sidedness we see in many political and environmental debates. Provoking self-justification reflexes in others presents a danger for advocates on all sides of an issue. An important key is to hold our beliefs lightly, said Carol Tavris, so if evidence comes along suggesting we might be wrong, we can give them up without feeling like idiots.

✦ ✦ ✦ ✦ ✦

It is hard to know who and what to believe, because our polarized world is driven by so much mistrust; PR campaigns are also waging a war on objectivity and sincerity. The public is being shown a picture of a world where everyone is trying to manipulate everyone else for their own gain, where no one can believe what they hear and where there is no possibility of objectivity. This atmosphere breeds mistrust and disinterest and crushes any hope of honest debate, noted Jason Stanley.

Phrases such as *ethical oil* or *clean coal* appear to be intentionally misleading and were never coined to persuade more than a handful of people. But intentional or not, outlandish allegations and improbable statements damage everyone's perception of sincerity and destroy opportunities for honest dialogue. For deliberative democracy to exist, we need to be more wary of campaigns delivering slick messages, of people who massage data to suit flawed ideological agendas or attack the credibility of experts.

The problem is worsened because humans are pre-wired to band into groups that share common sets of values and morals, and as Jonathan Haidt pointed out, any direct attacks on such shared values are highly polarizing because they cause open-minded thinking to shut down. By draining off passion, by recognizing that everyone has something of value to contribute, our awareness shifts and discussions can move beyond a perceived battle between good and evil. Stepping outside righteous attitudes even for a short while, by trying to understand another's point of view or reasoning, improves communication and helps us become more civil and open-minded with one another.

Propaganda campaigns play a role in public confusion about issues, and there is a powerful force that allows it to work. That force is *cultural cognition*: the tendency of individuals to conform their beliefs about matters of fact to values that define their cultural identities. We tend to look for evidence that confirms what we already believe, and that can lead to narrow-mindedness, partisan attitudes and noise in the public square. Dan Kahan explained that cultural cognition can lead some members of the public to disagree, sharply and persistently, about facts on which legions of experts and scientists agree. Greater awareness about our willingness to be misled can help us avoid misunderstandings and guide us to communicate more effectively and sensitively. We must understand the communication problems we face before we can find communication solutions.

The tendency to shape evidence and facts to our cultural identity works through unconscious forces of *confirmation bias* and *motivated reasoning*. The former is a type of selective thinking where we tend to notice and look for what confirms our beliefs. The latter makes us resist information that threatens our identity. It also drives people to develop elaborate rationalizations to justify their own beliefs, even when logic and evidence point in another direction. Rather than using narratives that threaten the values of others, Dan Kahan urged us to explore identity-affirming narratives and engage in more pluralistic advocacy so that diverse groups can arrive at truth within their own cultural values.

✦ ✦ ✦ ✦ ✦

As I began to look at narrative failure and why so many communication strategies lack impact, I started to learn more about the power of *moral dialogue*, which, if done well, can slice through barriers raised by polarization or propaganda. Many of us believe that if people have accurate, up-to-date information they will understand issues and come to the right conclusions. Certainly, facts and reason are fundamental to healthy public discourse, but in today's overheated adversarial public square facts are not enough. The sooner we recognize this the sooner we will reduce confusion.

Research coming from cognitive and brain science tells us if we want to be persuasive we must appeal to people's values and speak from a moral position, rather than layering on more data and statistics. George Lakoff warned that few people rely on empirical evidence to form their attitudes or to change their behavior. Too many facts, too much logic and too little emotion create confusion;

meaning becomes more elusive and arguments less persuasive. So as Lakoff explained, we need to get clear on our values, drop the language of policy and start using the emotional language of values.

Bruno Latour took this message a step further when he explained that fighting over facts does not to lead to public consensus or policy action; when everyone claims to speak in the name of truth, the result is gridlock. We desperately need healthy, lively debate, but when one or both sides claim the superiority of its facts, we close down debate rather than foster it. We can solve this impasse by encouraging debate about *matters of concern*, and by urging scientists not to cling to notions that they must remain impartial and just state the facts. Pure evidence is no basis for debate when the public is ill equipped to analyze all of the facts.

♦ ♦ ♦ ♦ ♦

The initial strategy in any kind of change process should be *inquiry*, said Peter Senge. It's the other's values that matter, not ours, so our first question should be, What motivates other people, their organization or society? The next step is to learn to *follow the energy*, to focus our communication on understanding what truly matters to people and how we might help them move ahead. Social systems thinking suggests we go where change is happening, to accelerate positive efforts and support organizations that are aggressively doing the right things. When we pool our best ideas and cooperate with each other we start to operate differently.

New realities are created when we connect with the realm of possibilities and are inspired by fresh ways of operating, co-creating and communicating. Waking up to deeper levels of awareness allows us to transform our thinking and connect with our best futures. Otto Scharmer explained that shifts happen when minds and hearts open; when we begin to walk in others' shoes; when we have the will to let go and let come.

Greater *awareness* is essential, because the success of our actions depends less on what we do, or how we do it, than on the inner place from which we operate. We cannot transform a system's behavior until we transform the quality of awareness and actions of people within the system.

We also need to practice *generative and empathetic listening*. This superior skill is critical in any profession or endeavor, and especially whenever there is a culture clash or breakdown in social or economic systems. Genuine listening moves us away from judgments and allows something new to happen, something that hasn't quite manifested yet. When we deepen our listening, we engage in real conversations.

✦ ✦ ✦ ✦ ✦

I learned an enormous amount from Marshall Ganz who emphasized the power of *emotional dialogue*; it can give agency and deeper meaning to a cause as well as to those involved in it. We need to speak from the heart and open up conversations about shared values and how deeply we feel about a problem. A person may be the best speaker in the world, but if they get this part wrong they will fail.

✦ ✦ ✦ ✦ ✦

Powerful stories are best crafted around specific details of real events. Challenges or threats can create dissonance and anxiety, but a thoughtful public speaker balances these challenges with a message of hope that can spur action and evoke an experience of optimism and intention rather than dread, self-doubt and despair. We mobilize action when we embark upon a dialogue of the heart.

Weak storytelling skills and an over-reliance on facts can leave listeners indifferent and apathetic, whereas a well-crafted public narrative that evolves in the telling can point to a better future. The secret is to speak in a manner that touches hearts and helps us recognize who we really are and what we stand for, so that we can access inner courage and find a hopeful path forward.

A well-crafted public narrative helps tear down barriers of propaganda and polarization. This theme of emotional communication is grounded in the Golden Rule of treating others the way we want to be treated, with understanding, respect and compassion. When we practice such communication it creates what Karen Armstrong called a "virtuous cycle."

✦ ✦ ✦ ✦ ✦

There is nothing wrong with speaking out loudly about injustice. In fact, when it comes to the enormous problems facing humanity in these times, it is an urgent responsibility. Citizens in the Western world, who enjoy the benefits of great democracies, have a solemn duty to speak up and shed light on forces of corruption, deception and indifference that may undermine authentic public conversations and real change.

But the goal of public discourse should be to encourage participation and expose the truth, not to discourage opposition or crush those who disagree. Vigorous public debate is vital, but as Thich Nhat Hanh advised: "Speak the truth but not to punish." He reminded us that we need to learn to police our attitudes and develop a greater capacity for self-awareness and self-control because people who monitor their attitudes towards others, and don't allow resentment to flare, can actually hear what others are saying and begin to communicate.

Thich Nhat Hahn's statement that we should "speak the truth but not to punish" means practicing nonviolent speech. Gandhi too believed in bringing about social and political change through what he called Ahimsa, causing no injury to others through deed or word. Bryant Welch echoed the wisdom of this: When a victim of a verbal attack remains silent rather than responding aggressively in kind, it is much harder for the perpetrator to justify and thereby sustain their aggression. Their negativity is left to stew in its own ugliness, and the door to the real story perhaps opens up.

A wonderful example of grand, moral narrative is Pope Francis's 2015 Encyclical.[1] The papal warning about "unprecedented destruction of ecosystems"[2] is a beautifully crafted call to action that con-

tains almost all the elements of storytelling I have been writing
about. The encyclical speaks to humanity's deeper values, to our
sense of place and our humanity and our moral responsibility. This
heartfelt narrative is about the environment, but the style of this
urgent appeal could be a model for drawing people together and
motivating them to consider any important issue.

Pope Francis framed his issues at the outset by saying he would
like to "enter into dialogue with all people about our common
home."[3] He explained that he chose St. Francis of Assisi as his inspiration and namesake because the 13th-Century mystic was the
patron saint of all who study and work in the area of ecology, a pil-
grim who lived in simplicity and harmony with nature.[4] The Pope
went on to describe a shared challenge, a choice that must be made
in response to a threat, and while he outlined a desperate situation
he offered real hope by urging people to reconnect with the natural
world. He wrote,

> If we approach nature and the environment without this
> openness to awe and wonder, if we no longer speak the
> language of fraternity and beauty in our relationship with
> the world, our attitude will be that of masters, consumers,
> ruthless exploiters, unable to set limits on their immediate
> needs. By contrast, if we feel intimately united with all that
> exists, then sobriety and care will well up spontaneously. The
> poverty and austerity of Saint Francis were no mere veneer
> of asceticism, but something much more radical: a refusal to
> turn reality into an object simply to be used and controlled.[5]

> It is not enough, however, to think of different species merely
> as potential "resources" to be exploited, while overlooking
> the fact that they have value in themselves. Each year sees
> the disappearance of thousands of plant and animal species,
> which we will never know, which our children will never see,
> because they have been lost for ever. The great majority be-

come extinct for reasons related to human activity. Because of us, thousands of species will no longer give glory to God by their very existence, nor convey their message to us. We have no such right.[6]

We must regain the conviction that we need one another, that we have a shared responsibility for others and the world, and that being good and decent are worth it. We have had enough of immorality and the mockery of ethics, goodness, faith and honesty. It is time to acknowledge that light-hearted superficiality has done us no good. When the foundations of social life are corroded, what ensues are battles over conflicting interests, new forms of violence and brutality, and obstacles to the growth of a genuine culture of care for the environment.[7]

Following the release of the Pope's encyclical and his visit to the United States, a national study was conducted by Yale's School of Forestry and the Environment. It was called *The Francis Effect*,[8] and the report found more Americans and more American Catholics concerned about global warming than six months earlier. It also found an increasing number of Americans thinking of global warming as a moral issue and a social fairness issue that will harm people. In some cases the rise in awareness was as much as 20 percentage points.

Clearly this kind of grand moral message is effective. It can actually change minds, persuade and move people. Such moral narratives can cut through the polarized, polluted conversations we struggle with these days. Speaking from the heart, as well as with frankness, ethical conviction and reasonableness, allows people to connect with the real meaning. This echoes the wisdom of Thich Nhat Hanh when he said "speak the truth but not to punish."

We need to treat the public square with great respect, as the sacred place that it is, and if we seek change we should learn to use speech for its highest purpose—moral discourse. We have no right to do otherwise.

Endnotes

Prologue

1. DeSmog Blog. [online] [cited November 24, 2015] desmogblog.com.
2. James Hoggan and Richard Littlemore. *Climate Cover-Up: The Crusade to Deny Global Warming.* Greystone, 2009.
3. Dan Kahan, personal communication.
4. Eric Johnson, personal communication.
5. Deborah Tannen. "We need higher quality outrage." *Christian Science Monitor*, October 22, 2004. [online] [cited January 19, 2016] csmonitor.com/2004/1022/p09s01-coop.html.
6. "Among abstracts that expressed a position on AGW [Anthropogenic, or human-caused, Global Warming], 97.1% endorsed the scientific consensus. Among scientists who expressed a position on AGW in their abstract, 98.4% endorsed the consensus." See: J. Cook, et al. Quantifying the consensus on anthropogenic global warming in the scientific literature. *Environmental Research Letters*, Vol. 83#2 (2013). [online] [cited December 29, 2015] DOI:10.1088/1748-9326/8/2/024024.
7. Basques mourn symbolic oak tree. *BBC News*, April 22, 2004. [online] [cited December 16, 2015] news.bbc.co.uk/2/hi/europe/3649397.stm.

Chapter 1

1. Viewpoint Learning. "About Us—Daniel Yankelovich." [online] [cited October 7, 2015] viewpointlearning.com/about-us/who-we-are/daniel-yankelovich.
2. Viewpoint Learning. "About Us—Steven Rosell." [online] [cited October 7, 2015] viewpointlearning.com/about-us/who-we-are/steven-rosell.
3. James Hoggan, *Climate Cover-Up.*

4. Source for quotations in this and following paragraphs: Steve Rosell and Daniel Yankelovich, personal communication.

5. Daniel Yankelovich. "Across the red-blue divide: How to start a conversation." *Christian Science Monitor*, October 15, 2004. [online] [cited October 8, 2015] csmonitor.com/2004/1015/p10s02-coop .html.

Chapter 2

1. Unless otherwise specified, source for all quotations in this chapter: Roger Conner, personal communication.

2. Roger Conner. "Strategy and Stance: A Framework for Understanding Public Advocacy." *SSRN Electronic Journal* #11 (2005). [online] [cited October 20, 2015] researchgate.net/publication/228195710 _Strategy_and_Stance_A_Framework_for_Understanding_Public _Advocacy.

Chapter 3

1. David Brooks. *The Social Animal: The Hidden Sources of Love, Character, and Achievement.* Random House, 2012.

2. Carol Tavris and Elliot Aronson. *Mistakes Were Made (but Not by Me): Why We Justify Foolish Beliefs, Bad Decisions and Hurtful Acts,* 2nd rev. ed. Pinter & Martin, 2013.

3. Unless otherwise specified, source for all quotations in this chapter: Carol Tavris, personal communication.

4. Ola Svenson. "Are we all less risky and more skillful than our fellow drivers?" *Acta Psychologica.* Vol. 47#2 (1980), pp 143–148 [online] [cited January 19, 2016] DOI: 10.1016/0001-6918(81)90005-6. heatherlench.com/wp-content/uploads/2008/07/svenson.pdf.

5. Ifat Maoz, Andrew Ward, Michael Katz and Lee Ross. "Reactive Devaluation of an "Israeli" vs. "Palestinian" Peace Proposal." *The Journal of Conflict Resolution*, Vol. 46#4 (2002), pp. 515–546. [online] [cited: November 28, 2015] jcr.sagepub.com/content/46/4/515.

Chapter 4

1. Source for all quotations in this chapter: Jonathan Haidt, personal communication.

2. Jesse Graham, Brian A. Nosek and Jonathan Haidt. "The Moral

Stereotypes of Liberals and Conservatives: Exaggeration of Differences across the Political Spectrum." *PLoS ONE*, Vol. 7#12 (2012). [online] [cited November 28, 2015] doi:10.1371/journal.pone .0050092; journals.plos.org/plosone/article?id=10.1371/journal.pone .0050092. You can participate in their research and find out more about your own moral foundations at: yourmorals.org.

3. Jonathan Haidt. "The moral roots of liberals and conservatives." TED talk, March 2008. [online] [cited October 14, 2015] ted.com /talks/jonathan_haidt_on_the_moral_mind.

4. Jonathan Haidt. *The Righteous Mind: Why Good People Are Divided by Politics and Religion*. Vintage, 2013.

5. Gary Marcus. *Birth of the Mind: How a Tiny Number of Genes Creates the Complexity of Human Thought*. Basic Books, 2004, p. 34.

6. Attributed to Sengcan (Seng Ts'an), Arthur Waley (trans.) "On Trust in the Heart." in Edward Conze (ed.) *Buddhist Texts Through the Ages*. New York: Philosophical Library, 1954, pp. 296–298.

7. Jesse Graham et al. "Moral Foundations Theory: The Pragmatic Validity of Moral Pluralism." *Advances in Experimental Social Psychology*, Vol. 47 (2013), pp. 55–130. [online] [cited: November 28, 2015] bcf.usc.edu/~jessegra/papers/GHKMIWD.inpress.MFT.AESP .pdf.

8. Al Gore. *An Inconvenient Truth*, directed by David Guggenheim. Paramount, 2006. [online] [cited October 14, 2015] takepart.com/an -inconvenient-truth/film.

9. Gretchen Livingston. "Fewer than half of U.S. kids today live in a 'traditional' family." *Pew Research Centre Fact Tank*, December 22, 2014. [online] [cited January 19, 2016] pewresearch.org/fact-tank /2014/12/22/less-than-half-of-u-s-kids-today-live-in-a-traditional -family.

10. Matthew 7:3–5, Luke 6:41–42.

Chapter 5

1. Dan M. Kahan et al. "Cultural Cognition of Scientific Consensus." *Journal of Risk Research*, Vol. 14#2 (2011), pp. 147–74. [online] [cited November 29, 2015] dx.doi.org/10.2139/ssrn.1549444.

2. Unless otherwise specified, source for all quotations in this chapter: Dan Kahan, personal communication.

3. Dan M. Kahan et al. "Motivated Numeracy and Enlightened Self-Government." Yale Law School, Public Law Working Paper #307, September 3, 2013. [online] [cited October 15, 2015] culturalcognition.net/browse-papers/motivated-numeracy-and-enlightened-self-government.html.

4. Dan M. Kahan et al. "Biased Assimilation, Polarization, and Cultural Credibility: An Experimental Study of Nanotechnology Risk Perceptions." Harvard Law School Program on Risk Regulation, Research Paper #08-25 (2008). [online] [cited November 30, 2015] dx.doi.org/10.2139/ssrn.1090044.

5. Dan M. Kahan et al. "The polarizing impact of science literacy and numeracy on perceived climate change risks." *Nature Climate Change* Vol. 2 (2012), pp. 732–735. [online] [cited October 15, 2015] nature.com/nclimate/journal/v2/n10/full/nclimate1547.html.

6. Dan M. Kahan et al. "Cultural Cognition of Scientific Consensus."

Chapter 6

1. Unless otherwise specified, source for all quotations in this chapter: George Lakoff, personal communication.

2. John Harding. "10 million scallops are dead; Qualicum company lays off staff." *Parksville Qualicum Beach News*, February 25, 2015. [online] [cited October 15, 2015] pqbnews.com/news/247092381.html.

3. Damian Carrington. "Q&A: 'Climategate.'" *The Guardian*, November 22, 2011. [online] [cited October 15, 2015] theguardian.com/environment/2010/jul/07/climate-emails-question-answer.

4. George Lakoff. *Don't Think of an Elephant!: Know Your Values and Frame the Debate*. Chelsea Green, 2004, p. 19.

5. George Lakoff. *Whose Freedom? The Battle Over America's Most Important Idea*. Picador, 2007, p. 16.

Chapter 7

1. Unless otherwise specified, source for all quotations in this chapter: Bruno Latour, personal communication.

2. Bruno Latour and Steve Woolgar. *Laboratory Life: The Construction of Scientific Facts*. Princeton, 1986; Bruno Latour. *Pandora's Hope: Essays on the Reality of Science Studies*. Harvard, 1999; Bruno Latour.

We Have Never Been Modern. Harvard, 1993; Bruno Latour. *Science in Action: How to Follow Scientists and Engineers Through Society.* Harvard, 1988; Bruno Latour. *Politics of Nature: How to Bring the Sciences into Democracy.* Harvard, 2004.

3. Holberg Prize website. Bruno Latour wins the 2013 Holberg Prize. [online] [cited October 16, 2015] holbergprisen.no/en/holberg-prize -2013.html.

4. Bruno Latour. "From Realpolitik to Dingpolitik—An Introduction to Making Things Public." *Pavilion Journal for Politics and Culture* #15 (2010), [online] [cited October 16, 2015] pavilionmagazine.org /bruno-latour-from-realpolitik-to-dingpolitik-or-how-to-make -things-public.

5. Ibid.

6. Clive Hamilton. *Requiem for a Species: Why We Resist the Truth About Climate Change.* Earthscan, 2010.

7. Walter Lippmann. *The Phantom Public.* Transaction, 1993.

8. Robert Proctor and Londo Schiebinger, eds. *Agnotology: The Making and Unmaking of Ignorance.* Stanford, 2008.

Chapter 8

1. Joel Bakan. *The Corporation: The Pathological Pursuit of Profit and Power.* Free Press, 2005.

2. *The Corporation,* directed by Mark Achbar and Jennifer Abbott. Zeitgeist films, 2005, DVD.

3. Unless otherwise specified, source for all quotations in this chapter: Joel Bakan or Noam Chomsky, personal communication.

4. Leo E. Strine Jr. "The dangers of denial: The Need for a Clear-Eyed Understanding of the Power and Accountability Structure Established by the Delaware General Corporation Law." Wake Forest Law Review. Inst for Law & Econ Research Paper #15-08 (2015). [online] [cited December 3, 2015] ssrn.com/abstract=2576389.

5. Judith Lavoie. "Enbridge depiction of clear tanker route sparks outrage." Canadian Press, August 15, 2012. [online] [cited October 20, 2015] bc.ctvnews.ca/enbridge-depiction-of-clear-tanker-route -sparks-outrage-1.916234; Carol Linnitt. "LEAKED: Enbridge's New Northern Gateway Pipeline Ad Campaign 'Open to Better.'" DeSmogBlog, October 1, 2013. [online] [cited October 20, 2015]

desmog.ca/2013/10/01/leaked-enbridge-s-new-northern-gateway
-pipeline-ad-campaign-open-better.

6. American Legislative Exchange Council website. [online] [cited
   October 20, 2015] alec.org/.

Chapter 9

1. World Meteorological Organization. "WMO: 2015 likely to be
   Warmest on Record, 2011–2015 Warmest Five Year Period." Press
   Release, November 25, 2015. [online] [cited January 6, 2016] wmo
   .int/media/content/wmo-2015-likely-be-warmest-record-2011-2015
   -warmest-five-year-period.

2. Chris Cesare. "California snowpack lowest in past 500 years." *Nature News*, 2015. [online] [cited January 6, 2016] nature.com/news
   /california-snowpack-lowest-in-past-500-years-1.18345.

3. Rohit Inani. "More Than 2,300 People Have Now Died in India's
   Heat Wave." *Time*, June 2, 2015. [online] [cited January 6, 2016]
   time.com/3904590/india-heatwave-monsoon-delayed-weather
   -climate-change.

4. Kamran Haider and Khurrum Anis. "Heat Wave Death Toll Rises
   to 2,000 in Pakistan's Financial Hub." *Bloomberg*, June 23, 2015.
   [online] [cited January 6, 2016] bloomberg.com/news/articles
   /2015-06-24/heat-wave-death-toll-rises-to-2-000-in-pakistan-s
   -financial-hub.

5. NOAA National Centers for Environmental Information. "NOAA
   National Centers for Environmental Information, Global Analysis
   for November 2015." December 2015. [online] [cited January 6, 2016]
   ncdc.noaa.gov/sotc/global/201511.

6. World Meteorological Organization. "Hurricane Patricia is strongest
   recorded in Eastern North Pacific." WMO News, October 23, 2015.
   [online] [cited January 6, 2016] wmo.int/media/content/hurricane
   -patricia-strongest-recorded-eastern-north-pacific.

7. Alexandra Witze. "Corals worldwide hit by bleaching." *Nature News*,
   October 8, 2015. [online] [cited January 6, 2016] nature.com/news
   /corals-worldwide-hit-by-bleaching-1.18527.

8. CBC's Power & Politics with Evan Solomon, January 11, 2012.
   Pipeline Debate Heats Up. (2012) [online] [cited December 29, 2015]
   cbc.ca/player/play/2186004232.

9. CTV's Question Period: January 8, 2012. Kathryn Marshall debates

Northern Gateway. [online] [cited December 29, 2015] youtube.com /watch?v=KvIx_wimOlI.

10. Debates of the Senate, 41st Parl, 1st Sess, Volume 148, Issue 54 (February 28, 2012) at 1710 (Nicole Eaton). [online] [cited October 27, 2015] parl.gc.ca/Content/Sen/Chamber/411/Debates/054db _2012-02-28-e.htm#70.

11. Canadian Press. "Environmental charities don't top list of foreign-funded groups." CBC News, May 10, 2012. [online] [cited October 20, 2015] cbc.ca/news/politics/environmental-charities-don-t-top -list-of-foreign-funded-groups-1.1247417.

12. Canadian Press. "Canadian charities in limbo as tax audits widen to new groups." CBC News, July 10, 2014. [online] [cited October 20, 2015] cbc.ca/news/politics/canadian-charities-in-limbo-as-tax -audits-widen-to-new-groups-1.2703177.

13. Debates of the Senate, 41st Parl, 1st Sess, Vol. 148 Issue 105 (October 3, 2012) at 1440 (Donald Neil Plett) [online] [cited January 20, 2016] parl.gc.ca/content/sen/chamber/411/debates/105db_2012-10-03-e .htm

14. *The Big Chill: Silencing Public Interest Science, A Survey*. Professional Institute of the Public Service of Canada, n.d. [online] [cited October 20, 2015] bigchill.en.pdf.

15. The author's Sustainability Research Initiative surveyed 10,000 Canadians on their opinions. Eighty percent rated environmental sustainability as a top or high priority: Hoggan website. "Sustainability Research." [online] [cited December 28, 2015] hoggan.com /Sustainability-Research.

16. Joanne Richard. "Pumping up the volume; Sun News Presents Ezra Levant." *The Calgary Sun*. December 26, 2011. Republished by ezralevant.com. [online] [cited December 29, 2015] ezralevant.com /pumping_up_the_volume.

17. Ezra Levant. *Ethical Oil: The Case for Canada's Oil Sands*. McClelland and Stewart, 2010, pp. 233–4.

18. CBC's Power & Politics with Evan Solomon, January 11, 2012.

19. See a website by the same name: [online] [cited October 21, 2015] exxonhatesyourchildren.com/learnmore.html.

20. Ezralevant.com. "Ethical Oil in the Globe and Mail again." January 15, 2011. [online] [cited December 29, 2015] ezralevant.com/ethical _oil_in_the_globe_and_m/.

21. Conference Board of Canada. *Environment.* [online] [cited October 21, 2015] conferenceboard.ca/hcp/details/environment.aspx.

22. World Wildlife Fund. "Canada ranked last in G8 on climate action." July, 2009. [online] [cited December 29, 2015] wwf.ca/newsroom /?4000.

23. Ramez Naam. "Arctic Sea Ice: What, Why and What Next?" *Scientific American Blog,* September 21, 2012. [online] [cited December 29, 2015] blogs.scientificamerican.com/guest-blog/arctic-sea-ice-what -why-and-what-next/

24. Bill C-38, Jobs, Growth and Long-Term Prosperity Act, 1st Sess., 41st Parl, 2012 (as amended 24 September 2014). [online] [cited October 27, 2015] canlii.ca/t/8qvz.

25. Jodi Stark. "Forty per cent of Australian oceans protected—What about Canada?" *David Suzuki Foundation Blog,* June 14, 2012. [online] [cited December 29, 2015] davidsuzuki.org/blogs/healthy-oceans -blog/2012/06/australia-protects-40-per-cent.

26. Jesse Coleman. "LEAKED: What you should know about Edelman and TransCanada's attack plan." *Greenpeace Blog,* November 14, 2014. [online] [cited December 29, 2015] greenpeace.org/usa/leaked -edelman-transcanadas-pr-attack-plan/.

27. Shawn McCarthy. "Greenpeace sees dirty tricks in PR Firms Trans-Canada Plan." *The Globe and Mail,* November 17, 2014. [online] [cited December 29. 2015] theglobeandmail.com/report-on-business /industry-news/energy-and-resources/greenpeace-sees-dirty-tricks -in-pr-firms-transcanada-plan/article21630761/.

28. Edelman. "TC Energy East: Grassroots Advocacy Vision Document." May 15, 2014. [online] [cited December 29, 2015] assets.document cloud.org/documents/1362369/tc-energy-east-grassroots-advocacy -vision-document.pdf.

29. Richard Edelman. "A Commitment." *Edelman 6 A.M. Blog,* October 16, 2006. edelman.com/p/6-a-m/a-commitment/; Pallavi Gogoi. "Wal-Mart's Jim and Laura: The Real Story." *Bloomberg Business,* October 9, 2006. bloomberg.com/bw/stories/2006-10-09/wal -marts-jim-and-laura-the-real-storybusinessweek-business-news -stock-market-and-financial-advice: Both [online] [cited December 29, 2015]

30. Brendan DeMelle. "Lobbyists for Big Oil Organizing Most 'Grass-roots' 'Energy Citizens' Rallies." *DeSmogBlog*, August 24, 2009. [online] [cited October 21, 2015] desmogblog.com/directory/vocabulary/4451.

31. Kate Sheppard. "Here's What Big Oil Has In The Pipes If Keystone Fails." *HuffingtonPost*, November 17, 2014. [online] [cited December 29, 2015] huffingtonpost.com/2014/11/17/transcanada-pipeline-oil_n_6174570.html.

32. Edward Walker. *Grassroots for Hire: Public Affairs Consultants in American Democracy*. Cambridge University Press, 2014.

33. Eric Lipton. "Hard-Nosed Advice From Veteran Lobbyist: 'Win Ugly or Lose Pretty'—Richard Berman Energy Industry Talk Secretly Taped" *New York Times*, October 30, 2014. [online] [cited October 21, 2015] nytimes.com/2014/10/31/us/politics/pr-executives-western-energy-alliance-speech-taped.html.

34. Hoggan, *Climate Cover-up*, p. 32.

35. Christopher Stevens. "The pea souper that killed 12,000: How the Great Smog choked London 60 years ago this week." *The Daily Mail*, December 6, 2012. [online] [cited December 29, 2015] dailymail.co.uk/news/article-2243732/Pea-souper-killed-12-000-So-black-screen-cinemas-So-suffocatingly-lethal-ran-coffins-How-Great-Smog-choked-London-60-years-ago-week.html#ixzz3vlK4wtBV.

36. This is down from 24,000 deaths in 2004 due to stricter regulations and enforcement: Clean Air Task Force. "Death and Disease from Power Plants." 2010. [online] [cited December 29, 2015] catf.us/fossil/problems/power_plants.

37. Union of Concerned Scientists. "Environmental impacts of coal power: air pollution." [online] [cited December 29, 2015] ucsusa.org/clean_energy/coalvswind/co2c.html.

38. Richard Conniff. "The Myth of Clean Coal." *Yale Environment 360*, June 3, 2008. [online]. [cited December 29, 2015]. e360.yale.edu/feature/the_myth_of_clean_coal/2014.

39. Brendan DeMelle. "ACCCE Coal Lobby Drops Bonner & Associates Over Forged Letters." *DeSmogBlog*, August 21, 2009. [online] [cited October 22, 2015] desmogblog.com/accce-coal-lobby-drops-bonner-associates-over-forged-letters.

Chapter 10

1. Unless othrwise specified, source for all quotations in this chapter: Alex Himelfarb, personal communication.

2. Since 2005, Hoggan & Associates has participated in a series of on-going surveys and dialogue-based research studies on the Canadian public's understanding, values and attitudes toward sustainability. Findings suggest that a strong majority of Canadians say climate change is very serious, is happening now and receives inadequate action from Canada's leaders, and that government and business should address both economic and environmental challenges as a top priority and support addressing the growing gap between rich and poor as a social injustice. Participants identified three key barriers to acting more sustainably: mistrust of government and business; belief that individual actions have no meaningful impact on the big picture; and lack of reliable, relevant information. More about the studies and their findings are available here: Hoggan website. "Sustainability Research."

3. "Margaret Thatcher in Quotes." *The Spectator*, April 8, 2013. [online] [cited October 26, 2015] blogs.new.spectator.co.uk/2013/04/margaret-thatcher-in-quotes/.

4. Debra Marshall. "C. Wright Mills—The Sociological Imagination." YouTube, December 24, 2012. [online] [cited October 26, 2015] youtube.com/watch?v=dMR74ytkXKI.

5. Meagan Fitzpatrick. "Harper on terror arrests: Not a time for 'sociology.'" *CBC News*, April 25, 2013. [online] [cited October 26, 2015] cbc .ca/news/politics/harper-on-terror-arrests-not-a-time-for-sociology -1.1413502.

Chapter 11

1. Jason Stanley, "Democracy and the Demagogue." *New York Times*, October 12, 2015. [online] [cited October 26, 2015] opinionator.blogs .nytimes.com/author/jason-stanley/?_r=0.

2. Newshounds. "Fox News regular suggests Obama is a Muslim." YouTube, August 19, 2010. [online] [cited October 26, 2015] youtube .com/watch?v=qCog5l9kq94.

3. Unless otherwise specified, source for all quotations in this chapter: Jason Stanley, personal communication.

4. George Orwell. *Nineteen Eighty-Four*. Penguin Books, 1949.

5. Victor Klemperer, translated by Martin Chalmers. *I Shall Bear Witness: The Diaries of Victor Klemperer, 1933–41*. Weidenfeld & Nicolson, 1998; Victor Klemperer, translated by Martin Chalmers. *To the Bitter End: The Diaries of Victor Klemperer, 1942–1945*. Weidenfeld & Nicolson, 1999.

6. Ben Zimmer. "Truthiness." *The New York Times Magazine*, October 13, 2010. [online] [cited Decenmber 28, 2015] nytimes.com/2010/10/17/magazine/17FOB-onlanguage-t.html.

Chapter 12

1. Bryant Welch. *State of Confusion: Political Manipulation and the Assault on the American Mind*. Thomas Dunne, 2008.

2. *Gaslight* directed by George Cukor, MGM, 1944.

3. Unless otherwise specified, source for all quotations in this chapter: Bryant Welch, personal communication.

4. Stephen Colbert, 2006 White House Correspondents' Association Dinner. [online] [cited December 8, 2015] c-span.org/video/?192243-1/2006-white-house-correspondents-dinner.

5. Welch counts Karl Rove, Republican political consultant and former senior advisor and deputy chief of staff to George W. Bush, among America's most effective "gaslighters," influential people who actively create and exploit confusion in the minds of Americans. In *State of Confusion*, Welch casts Rove as the "creative genius" behind Bush's political success and discusses the many "tricks" he uses to manipulate the public; see pp. 122–128 and 133–134.

6. Franklin D. Roosevelt. "The only thing we have to fear is fear itself." Great Speeches of the 20th Century, *The Guardian*, April 25, 2007. [online] [cited October 28, 2015] theguardian.com/theguardian/2007/apr/25/greatspeeches.

Chapter 13

1. Mark Stoll. "Personal Attacks on Rachel Carson." *Rachel Carson's Silent Spring, A Book That Changed The World*. Environment and Society Portal, Virtual Exhibitions 2012 no. 1. [online] [cited October 30, 2015] environmentandsociety.org/exhibitions/silent-spring/personal-attacks-rachel-carson.

2. Deborah Tannen. "We need higher quality outrage." *The Christian Science Monitor*, October 20, 2004. [online] [cited: December 29, 2015] faculty.georgetown.edu/tannend/csm102204.html.

3. Source for all quotes in this paragraph: Bryant Welch, personal communication.

4. Onora O'Neill. *A Question of Trust, The BBC Reith Lectures*, 2002. Cambridge, 2002.

5. Equality and Human Rights Commission. "About Us." [online] [cited November 2, 2015] equalityhumanrights.com/about-us.

6. Source for all quotes of Baroness O'Neill: Baroness Onora O'Neill, personal communication.

7. "Marshall Ganz on Making Social Movements Matter." BillMoyers .com, May 10, 2013. [online] [cited November 2, 2015] billmoyers.com /segment/marshall-ganz-on-making-social-movements-matter.

8. Unless otherwise specified, source for all quotes in this and succeeding paragraphs: Marshall Ganz, personal communication.

9. On1Foot: Jewish Texts for Social Justice. "Arguing for the Sake of Heaven." Mishnah, *Pirkei Avot* 5:17. [online] [cited November 2, 2015] on1foot.org/sourcesheet/arguing-sake-heaven.

Chapter 14

1. Books by Adam Kahane: *Solving Tough Problems: An Open Way of Talking, Listening, and Creating New Realities.* Barrett-Koehler, 2007; *Power and Love: A Theory and Practice of Social Change.* Berrett-Koehler, 2010; *Transformative Scenario Planning: Working Together to Change the Future.* Berrett-Koehler, 2012.

2. Blurbs quoted from Kahane. Transformative Scenario Planning.

3. Source for all quotations from Adam Kahane in this chapter: Adam Kahane, personal communication.

4. Paul Tillich. *Love, Power, and Justice: Ontological Analyses and Ethical Applications.* Oxford, 1954.

5. Martin Luther King, Jr., edited by James Washington. *A Testament of Hope: The Essential Writings and Speeches of Martin Luther King, Jr.* HarperSanFrancisco, 1990, p. 247.

Chapter 15

1. American systems scientist Peter Senge is a major figure in the organizational development field. Senge was named Strategist of

the Century by the *Journal of Business Strategy*, and *Harvard Business Review* has referred to his vision of a learning organization in his 1990 book, *The Fifth Discipline*, as one of the seminal management ideas of the previous 75 years. See Peter Senge. *The Fifth Discipline: The Art and Practice of a Learning Organization*. Deckle Edge, 2006.

2. Source for all quotations from Peter Senge in this chapter: Peter Senge, personal communication.

3. For example, see Mike Gaworecki. "China To Create National Cap-And-Trade Program As Obama Admin Must Bypass U.S. Senate On Climate." *DeSmogBlog*, September 25, 2014. [online] [cited November 4, 2015] desmogblog.com/2014/09/23/china-create-national-cap-and-trade-program-obama-admin-must-bypass-u-s-senate-climate.

4. "Video Message from Xie Zhenhua, Vice Chairman of the National Development and Reform Commission (NDRC), China." Globe International Second Climate Legislation Summit, February 27–28, 2014. [online] [cited November 4, 2015] globelegislators.org/2gcls-proceedings/videomessage-from-xie-zhenhua-china.

5. Jack Clark. "IT now 10 percent of world's electricity consumption, report finds." *The Register*, August 16, 2013. [online] [cited November 4, 2015] theregister.co.uk/2013/08/16/it_electricity_use_worse_than_you_thought.

6. Paul Gilding. *The Great Disruption: Why the Climate Crisis Will Bring On the End of Shopping and the Birth of a New World*. Bloomsbury, 2012; Paul Gilding. "The Earth is full." TED 2012, February 2012. [online] [cited November 4, 2012] ted.com/talks/paul_gilding_the_earth_is_full.

Chapter 16

1. Willian J. O'Brien. *Character at Work: Building Prosperity Through the Practice of Virtue*. Paulist Press, 2008.

2. Source for all quotations from Otto Scharmer in this chapter: Otto Scharmer, personal communication.

3. Otto Scharmer website. [online] [cited November 6, 2015] ottoscharmer.com; C. Otto Scharmer. *Theory U: Leading from the Future as It Emerges*. Berrett-Koehler, 2009; Otto Scharmer and Katrin Kaufer. *Leading from the Emerging Future: From Ego-System to Eco-System Economies*. Berrett-Koehler, 2013.

4. Source for all quotations from Anne Giardini in this chapter: Anne
   Giardini, personal communication.

5. Otto Scharmer. "Shaping the Future." World Econonic Forum,
   Tianjin, September 13–15, 2010. [online] [cited November 6, 2015]
   ottoscharmer.com/publications/videos.

Chapter 17

1. "Archive." Renee Lertzman website. [online] [cited November 6,
   2015] reneelertzman.com/archive.

2. Source for all quotations from Renee Lertzman in this chapter:
   Renee Lertzman, personal communication.

3. Harold F. Searles. "Unconscious Processes in Relation to the Environmental Crisis." *Psychoanalytic Review*. Vol. 59, (1972).

4. Hanna Segal. (1987, 1997) "Silence is the real crime" in Hanna Segal.
   Psychoanalysis, Literature and War: Papers 1942–1995. Routledge, 2005.

5. Kari Norgaard. *Living in Denial: Climate Change, Emotions, and
   Everyday Life*. MIT Press, 2011.

6. Renee Lertzman. "The myth of apathy." *The Ecologist*, June 19, 2008.
   [online] [cited: December 25, 2015] theecologist.org/blogs_and
   _comments/commentators/other_comments/269433/the_myth_of
   _apathy.html.

Chapter 18

1. Paul Slovic biography. Decision Research website. [online] [cited
   November 9, 2015] decisionresearch.org/researcher/paul-slovic-ph-d.

2. Source for all quotations from Paul Slovic in this chapter: Paul
   Slovic, personal communication.

3. United Human Rights Council. "Genocide in Darfur." [online] [cited
   November 9, 2015] unitedhumanrights.org/genocide/genocide-in
   -sudan.htm.

4. Paul Slovic and Elke U. Weber. "Perception of Risk Posed by Extreme Events." Paper prepared for discussion at the conference "Risk
   Management strategies in an Uncertain World," Palisades, New York,
   April 12–13, 2002. [online] [cited November 9, 2015] ldeo.columbia
   .edu/chrr/documents/meetings/roundtable/white_papers/slovic
   _wp.pdf.

5. Paul Slovic. *The Feeling of Risk: New Perspectives on Risk Perception*.
   Routledge, 2010.

6. Daniel Kahneman. *Thinking, Fast and Slow.* Farrar, Straus and Giroux, 2013.
7. Daniel Kahneman, Paul Slovic and Amos Tversky, eds. *Judgment Under Uncertainty: Heuristics and Biases.* Cambridge, 1982.

Chapter 19
1. Source for all quotations from Marshall Ganz in this chapter: Marshall Ganz, personal communication.

Chapter 20
1. "Karen Armstrong Religious scholar." Speakers, TED.com. [online] [cited November 11, 2015] ted.com/speakers/karen_armstrong.
2. Source for all quotations from Karen Armstrong in this chapter: Karen Armstrong, personal communication.
3. Source for all quotations from Joan Halifax in this chapter: Joan Halifax, personal communication.
4. 1 Corinthians 13: 4 and 6.

Chapter 21
1. Source for all quotations from Thich Nhat Hanh in this chapter: Thich Nhat Hanh, retreat and interview, Awakening the Heart Retreat, UBC, August 8–13, 2011.
2. Peter Solomon in "Happiness Machines," Episode One, *The Century of Self*, BBC Two England, 2002.
3. A Zen koan is a "succinct paradoxical statement or question used as a meditation discipline for novices, particularly in the Rinzai sect. The effort to 'solve' a koan is intended to exhaust the analytic intellect and the egoistic will, readying the mind to entertain an appropriate response on the intuitive level. Each such exercise constitutes both a communication of some aspect of Zen experience and a test of the novice's competence." See "koan." *Encyclopædia Britannica Online.* Encyclopædia Britannica Inc., 2016. [online] [cited January 20, 2016] britannica.com/topic/koan.

Chapter 22
1. John Esposito. "The Global Implications of Tibetan Interdependence." *Asian Journal of Global Studies.* Vol 5#1 (2013). [online] [cited February 2, 2016] ajgs.org/index.php/AJGS/article/view/102/133.

2. Barry Saxifrage. "Wikileak: Dalai Lama says climate change in Tibet more urgent than political solution. Why?" *Vancouver Observer,* January 25, 2011. [online] [cited December 26, 2015] vancouverobserver .com/blogs/climatesnapshot/2011/01/25/wikileak-dalai-lama-says -climate-change-tibet-more-urgent-political; World Wildlife Fund. "Glaciers In China And Tibet Fading Fast." *Science Daily,* February 22, 2009. [online] [cited December 26, 2015] sciencedaily.com/releases /2009/02/090220185537.htm.

3. Baiqing Xu et al. "Black soot and the survival of Tibetan glaciers." *Proceedings* of the National Academies of Sciences. Vol. 106#52 (2009). [online] [cited December 25, 2015] pnas.org/content/106/52 /22114.full.pdf; James Hansen. "Science Briefs: Survival of Tibetan Glaciers." NASA GISS Website, December 2009. [online] [cited December 25, 2015] giss.nasa.gov/research/briefs/hansen_14.

4. Future Generations China. "Four Great Rivers Project." [online] [cited November 17, 2015] china.future.org/conservation-tibet/four -great-rivers.

5. Claudio O. Delang and Zhen Yuan. *China's Grain for Green Program: A Review of the Largest Ecological Restoration and Rural Development Program in the World.* Springer, 2014.

6. Mind and Life Conference XXIII. [online] [cited November 18, 2015] mindandlife.org/dalai-lama-dialogues.

7. Source for all quotations of the 14th Dalai Lama in this chapter: The 14th Dalai Lama, retreat and interview, Mind and Life Conference XXIII: Ecology, Ethics, and Interdependence. Office of His Holiness the Dalai Lama, October 17–21, 2011.

8. Source for all quotations of Sally McFague in this chapter: Sally McFague, personal communication.

9. Source for all quotations of Peter Senge in this chapter: Peter Senge, personal communication.

Epilogue

1. Pope Francis. *Encyclical Letter Laudato Si' of the Holy Father Francis On Care For* Our Common Home. May 24, 2015. [online] [cited November 30, 2015] w2.vatican.va/content/francesco/en/encyclicals /documents/papa-francesco_20150524_enciclica-laudato-si.html.

2. Ibid, para. 24.

3. Ibid. para. 3.

4. Ibid. para. 10.

5. Ibid. para. 11.

6. Ibid. para. 33.

7. Ibid. para 229.

8. E. Maibach et al. *The Francis Effect: How Pope Francis Changed the Conversation about Global Warming.* George Mason University and Yale University, 2015. [online] [cited January 8, 2016] environment .yale.edu/climate-communication/files/The_Francis_Effect.pdf.

Index

About the Author

JAMES HOGGAN is president of the PR firm Hoggan & Associates and chair of the David Suzuki Foundation board. A tireless advocate for ethics and integrity in public relations, he founded the influential website *DeSmogBlog* to expose misinformation campaigns that pollute public debate around climate change and the environment. He has advised a wide range of organizations, governments, universities and corporations, and is a sought-after speaker around North America and Europe. Hoggan has chaired and served on numerous national and international boards and advisory committees including the Four Great Rivers Society and Shell Global's External Review Committee. He is the author of *Climate Cover-Up* and *Do the Right Thing: PR Tips for a Skeptical Public*.

If you have enjoyed *I'm Right and You're an Idiot*, you might also enjoy other

BOOKS TO BUILD A NEW SOCIETY

Our books provide positive solutions for people who
want to make a difference. We specialize in:

Climate Change ◆ Conscious Community
Conservation & Ecology ◆ Cultural Critique
Education & Parenting ◆ Energy ◆ Food & Gardening
Health & Wellness ◆ Modern Homesteading & Farming
New Economies ◆ Progressive Leadership ◆ Resilience
Social Responsibility ◆ Sustainable Building & Design

For a full list of NSP's titles, please call 1-800-567-6772 *or check out our web site at:*

www.newsociety.com

The Emotions of Teacher Stress